WISHER,
WASHER

THIS BOOK IS GIVEN TO:

Name

because I believe in you!

GIVER'S NAME   DATE

PUBLISHED BY

PositivePsyche.Biz

13017 Wisteria Drive

Germantown, MD

United States of America

Copyright © 2014 by Enrique Ruiz

1st Edition

All rights reserved

Paperback: ISBN 978-0-989-88344-3

www.WisherWasher.com

LIBRARY OF CONGRESS CONTROL NUMBER:

2010909309

Other Products by Enrique Ruiz:

"Be A Washer" Action Guide

ISBN 978-0-9898834-4-3

www.BeAWasher.com

I Am Hurt Cards

ISBN 978-0-9827636-8-1

www.IAmHurt.biz

Love Adventure Game

ISBN 978-0-9827636-2-9

www.LoveAdventureGame.com

Lost Love

ISBN 978-0-9827636-1-2

www.LoveIsLost.com

www.positivepsyche.biz

DESIGN AND LAYOUT BY JENNIFER TYSON

www.leftrightcollaborative.com

There are only three kinds of people:

WISHERS,
WASHERS,
AND
WISHY-
WASHY'S

What kind of person are you?
Be a WASHER!

ENRIQUE RUIZ

positive
psyche

A PositivePsyche.biz Book
Maryland, U.S.A.

MOVE

"All mankind is divided into three classes:

those that are immovable,
those that are movable,
and those that move"

Ben Franklin

To our daughter Sasha (in remembrance),

my phenomenal wife Sarah

and our children

Shaina, Shaun, Hannah, Molly and André

"A strong, successful man is not the victim
of his environment. He creates favorable
conditions. His own inherent force and energy
compel things to turn out as he desires."

ORISON SWETT MARDEN
FOUNDER OF *SUCCESS* MAGAZINE

"You will become clever through your mistakes."

GERMAN PROVERB
AMERICAN WRITER AND POET

I have lived like a rich kid – *and* on the "other side of the tracks." Sometimes I thought I knew it all and that I was on the fast track. Other times my ignorance was glaringly obvious. But as I've read more and added life experiences, I've become wiser. Today, I have achieved a notable status in life – fancy titles, impressive paychecks and business success – and yet like so many others, I remain perpetually on the road to discovery and continued achievement.

Most people dream of success but, as they grow older, settle into believing that life got in the way, that their unfulfilled dreams and unachieved goals were simply not meant to be. I disagree. It is a matter of choice and of persistence, coupled with dogged determination in the face of obstacles, setbacks and failures. Success, when you've scaled the mountain and really earned it, is so much sweeter. And wishing for success and committing yourself to it are very different things.

Of course, "success" is a relative term. Each of us must determine which mountains we want to climb and set priorities based on the utility we want to bring to our families, companies and communities, and to society as a whole. Reaching those objectives is success. But the difference between ordinary and extraordinary is a little *extra*. What extra commitment will you make? What extra endeavor will you pursue? What extra sacrifices will you make?

This book blends time-tested philosophy with a host of modern-day tools for the psyche published in several personal development and business books – and exemplifies them through the story of one young man's life. (The character could just as easily have been a young lady, as these concepts are in no way gender specific, but to avoid using the awkward "he/she" throughout the book, I chose the masculine form.) Then, in the "Models, Movers and Mentors" section, you'll read about successful and inspirational men *and* women who've defied great odds and bounced back from repeated failures to change the world.

So, what difference will *your* difference make?

What People Are Saying
about *Wisher, Washer, Wishy-Washy*

If you have ever had the pleasure to meet Rick Ruiz in person you are immediately struck by the intriguing "twinkle" in his eyes — like he knows something you don't. As it turns out he does and he shares it with us in his book, "Wisher, Washer, Wishy-Washy." He has turned his extraordinary life lessons into an easily understood but powerful concept of introspective self evaluation and achievable action. His fictional approach to non-fictional self-help principles places you, the reader, in the story and, therefore, responsible for the ending — your success.

ED ARMSTRONG
RETIRED U.S. AIR FORCE COLONEL AND
LOCKHEED MARTIN MASTER PROGRAM MANAGERS

"This amazing book will totally help and inspire you."

KRISTI FRANK
AS SEEN ON *OPRAH*, MSNBC,
THE TODAY SHOW AND SEASON #1 OF *THE APPRENTICE*

"Without them, you do not even have a life. With these two attributes, you conquer the demons in your mind that prevent success in any walk of life. It's called a high reality level. Successful people in any endeavor, in all phases of life, require two prominent attributes: truth and honesty. Athletes, in particular, have a head start in coming to terms with themselves on a daily basis. When they apply truth and honesty to training, competing and life itself, they become true champions. They become Washers. This conclusion is based on more than 50 years of experience in coaching the sport of Track & Field at the local, national and international level. Wisher, Washer Wishy-Washy is a very high class book."

HARRY GROVES
TRACK & FIELD COACH TO 11 AMERICAN RECORD-HOLDERS, 21 NATIONAL CHAMPIONS,
14 OLYMPIANS AND 227 ALL AMERICANS

"[This is a] great book. It will power and inspire people to be better and to be more, do more and achieve more."

JAMES MALINCHAK
CO-AUTHOR OF THE BEST-SELLING BOOK
CHICKEN SOUP FOR THE COLLEGE SOUL
AND TWO-TIME "COLLEGE SPEAKER OF THE YEAR"

"As a former editor of PINK magazine, a national publication for business women, I've interviewed hundreds of experts and read many books, articles and studies on personal development, leadership, diversity and other tactics for success in business and in life. These are topics that I am passionate about, that I believe make or break the person, or the company, so it has been an honor to edit Wisher, Washer, Wishy-Washy, Enrique Ruiz's simple but engaging story of one man's life. In it, he takes the concepts that the world's most successful CEOs, innovators, athletes and scientists live by, the principles and ideas that have inspired best-selling business and personal development books, and presents them in a way that is accessible, engaging and relatable.

Who among us hasn't stumbled, looked for an easier path only to discover that fast tracks are often illusions or dead ends, or experienced a failure that could easily become a great excuse for giving up? But, as Ruiz's story beautifully illustrates, it's what we do after we fail, when we make the decision to learn and grow more with each hurdle, that we discover the secrets to our own personal definitions of success."

TAYLOR MALLORY
FOUNDER OF TAYLORED EDITORIAL

"This motivating, entertaining book gives you steps to take and a track to run on to achieve tremendous success in every area of your life."

BRIAN TRACY
WORLD-RENOWNED MOTIVATIONAL SPEAKER AND BEST-SELLING AUTHOR
OF *NO EXCUSES: THE PERSONAL SELF-DISCIPLINE*

"I liked this book. The format and presentation is easy to read and rich with content that is both practical and applicable to anyone's personal growth. There is also a depth in the subject matter that reflects the author's extensive knowledge of the growth process."

DR. BOB TURKNETT
AUTHOR OF *DECENT PEOPLE, DECENT COMPANY; HOW TO LEAD WITH CHARACTER AT WORK AND IN LIFE*
EXECUTIVE LEADERSHIP COACH AND LICENSED PSYCHOLOGIST WITH OVER
28 YEARS OF CONSULTING EXPERIENCE

"A common sense approach to analyzing events, choices and turning points in our own lives. Ruiz gives us common terms, with deep meaning, to help define our positions and quests in life."

DR. DENIS WAITLEY
AUTHOR OF *SEEDS OF GREATNESS*, HIGHLY SOUGHT-AFTER KEYNOTE LECTURER
AND PRODUCTIVITY CONSULTANT ON HIGH-PERFORMANCE HUMAN ACHIEVEMENT

In Wisher, Washer, Wishy-Washy, author Enrique Ruiz encourages readers to become successful by embracing their chosen destinies rather than falling through the cracks by becoming 'Wishy-Washy.' We all need to stand on our own two feet, ignore those who will point out how difficult the paths we have chosen are and that we are surely doomed to fail so why bother trying? Using a fictional example of a boy who grows to be a man, Ruiz points out all those moments in time when our lives could have changed course... Are we Wishers, those who talk and dream of becoming successful but never take action to get there? or are we Washers, men and women of action who embrace those special opportunities that come our way?

Ruiz presents readers with numerous stories about real people, dreamers who dared to dream and succeeded, and mingles them with some very inspiring quotes. This is an uplifting read that truly inspires us to be the best we can be.

Judge, Writers Digest 21st Annual Book Awards - 2013

Sampling of students reaction to the Wisher-Washer concept in school events:

o Not many things should bring me down. I should chase my dreams no matter how hard it seems. I will not give up easilly anymore. JJ

o I create my own future, and if I keep wishing about things and don't actually DO something, I will not be all I can be. Don't quit! I will keep on pushing and even if I fail, I will try even harder. DB

o I learned it's OK to wish, but be a Washer. I will stop trying to impress everyone else and take hold of my future and achieve my goals. JD

See more at www.WisherWasher.com/testimonials.php

PART 1: **THE STORY**

PART 2: **MODELS, MOVERS AND MENTORS**

PART 3: **YOUR TURN**

PART 1:
THE STORY

THE BEGINNING

One magnificent day, a delicate Child is born – a beautiful Child, to be ogled and cooed over by the Big People who witness this magnificent occasion. Everyone marvels at the softness and tenderness of this small being, and in this period of admiration, all seem to know without saying so that this fragile creature possesses great intrinsic power – the power to garner knowledge, to discover the yet unseen and to lead, do and be.

The Child's Mother, who lovingly carried the baby for nine months, nurturing all of his physical needs while he grew within the warm confines of her womb, shares a tired but proud smile with her husband. Their love and unity has spawned a new human being, one whose emerging experiences, thoughts, feelings and ideas will soon change the world.

• • • •

> "A baby is God's opinion that
> the world should go on."
> **CARL SANDBURG**
> AMERICAN WRITER AND POET

• • • •

A unique creation, yet the Child seems, on the surface, like an ordinary little boy. But those who peer deep into his tiny eyes see a unique pattern within his iris and fingerprints unlike any others on Earth. If these minute details are so unique, what other exclusive attributes does this Child possess? What peculiarities set him apart? Will they help or hinder him? Only time will tell.

For now, the Child's potential fate and power are fleeting thoughts to those who revere him, and the newness of his arrival consumes the day. The Big

People wonder and speculate while they wish greatness and much happiness for the Child. The Child smiles, and his Parents are filled with pride and amazement. This Child is, for now, the center of the universe for the family that has assumed the responsibility for raising him.

Warmth, love, food and shelter take center stage as the Child grows. Holding, tickling, laughing and caressing their baby are the Parents' new favorite pastimes.

However, the Child carries within him the heritage of his ancestors as well as the ability to look into the future and mold a new generation.

His Parents pray for privilege and blessings and wonder about the celestial alignment of the stars. What advantage will he have? What divine or astrological gifts will the heavens bestow?

••••

"The day, water, sun, moon, night – I do not have to purchase these things with money."

PLAUTUS
ROMAN PLAYWRIGHT

••••

Time ticks on. The sun and moon complete many dutiful cycles. The planets revolve, and the universe continues to expand. Change and growth are perpetual constants, and yet often imperceptible. Can you feel the Earth turn? Can you hear the stars sing?

CHARACTER EMERGENCE

The Child grows and begins to assimilate his surroundings – the unique environment, family and body that will give him the life and mobility to explore and grow. With a sense of wonder, trepidation, happiness, excitement, puzzlement and amazement, he begins to identify, polish and hone the attributes life has given him.

The Child is now ready to walk. He sees the Big People moving to and fro with ease and independence. He knows that he too can accomplish this task. He tries but falls. He persists with gentle pleas and coaching from his Parents but fails over and over again. Still, the Child, who doesn't yet know the meaning of failure, is determined. His patient Parents watch and wait with anticipation while he topples over time and time again. Maybe he hasn't yet acquired enough stability, they speculate, or perhaps his bones and muscles are not yet strong enough. The Child, unaware of any limitations, only knows that he will rest and try again tomorrow. Several sunsets light the sky aglow before he is successful, but before long, he's up and off – running around on his own two legs.

Seasons come and go, and the Child's environment appears to expand. There are new senses to take in, new appreciations, other children and people to marvel at, and new questions – lots of new questions.

Winter comes in the middle of the night, or so the Child believes. One morning, he awakes to a marvelous new sight – outside his bedroom window, everything is white! He wonders at this strange beauty, but his Parents' enthusiasm tells him that this is a fun day. They explain the inherent purity of the snow while allowing the Child to gently touch his first snowflake. He jerks back his hand at first, startled by its almost painful coldness, but forgets his insecurities while he witnesses, with amazement, the white material transform into water. He is perplexed and awed. It is magical.

His Parents bundle him up in bulky clothing he has never seen, even stuffing his hands into warm sock-like coverings called gloves. He feels big and awkward with all of these layers of clothes, but as his Parents open the door, letting the cold, brisk air hit his exposed nose and lips, he appreciates the warmth of his new clothes. This is different!

His laughing, smiling Parents, their excitement contagious, lead him outside. The Child can hardly wait to explore this new mystery that has made his Parents so happy. But as he steps off the porch, he starts to sink into the whiteness. Terrified, he reaches for his Parents, whose smiles assure him that he is safe, and they encourage him to venture farther.

His Mother grabs a handful of snow and gently compacts the soft flakes into a small, white rock – then throws it at his Father! The Child has been told to be careful with rocks and worries that his Father might be hurt, but his Father only laughs and teaches him to build a snowball to throw back at his Mother. This is fun!

After they've taken turns throwing snowballs at each other, his Parents say it's time to build his first "snowman." They show him how to gather the snow into a much bigger ball than the ones they had thrown at each other, starting with fistfuls and then rolling it along the ground until it's almost as tall as he is! He doesn't know where all of this is leading, but his zestful Parents have not yet led him wrong. He is in the game. He follows their lead and continues to build an even bigger ball. Then his Parents stack the two snowballs on top of each other. It is too tall for him to reach now, so he helps by bringing more snow to receptive hands. With his Mother's help, he creates one smaller ball, which she places on the very top. He doesn't understand this logic, but he has learned at an early age that he cannot always see what is intended by the loving direction of his Parents.

His Father leaves this family assembly and goes into the house "to get something." The Child, excited to know what comes next, watches the door, eagerly awaiting his Father's return. Soon his Father comes out with a bag of things, and the Child watches in awe as a well-placed scarf, hat, pieces of coal and carrot bring to life a portly, smiling snowman in his front yard. The Child screams and laughs as he jumps up and down, clapping his hands.

Next, his Mother lies down on the ground and moves her arms and legs from side to side. When she stands up, he marvels at the imprint her body has left. She calls it a "snow angel." He wants to try! His Father lowers him down next to her. As he sinks into the snow, he feels it hug the outline of his body. He laughs as fresh flakes land on his face and melt, tickling his skin. He opens his mouth and is surprised to find that the snowflakes taste like water!

After hours of play, his Parents insist it's time to go inside and warm up. The Child, flushed from running around, doesn't understand the meaning of this but obeys. Inside, he watches his Mother prepare hot chocolate. She places water in a pot on the stove. As the fire from the stove gently laps at the pot, the water starts to bubble. The Child stares at it, his mind spinning.

As he sits with his Parents by a crackling fire, sipping the thick, sweet chocolate drink, his body is exhausted, but his mind isn't. He can hardly contain himself as he repeats his favorite word over and over: "Why?"

Why does water fall from the sky? Why is the snow cold, white and soft? Why, when it melts, does it turn into water? Why does hot water bubble? Why do these bubbles turn into steam, and why does the water slowly disappear? Where does it go? Why does he float on water in a swimming pool? Why does he see his reflection at the river's edge? Why does he get so thirsty, and why is water so refreshing? Why does he sweat when he plays hard? Why does the Earth look so beautiful, with such great oceans? Why can big ships float on the water, but cars must stay on dry land? Why must he bathe in water every day? If it weren't for the toys in the bathtub, he knows he might just choose to skip this task.

His Parents do their best to answer questions and enlighten the Child about life. He soon learns that parents have agendas of their own. These may include safety, survival, career success, pleasure, love, marriage, education, family and the like. The Child looks across the fence and sees other parents with other agendas and families with other circumstances. Although the moon, sun and seasons can be relied on to appear on schedule, they change every day. And even though a million miles away, the sun touches our very skin. The Child soon learns that life in the people world is full of change and somehow has an impact on him.

Each night the Child's Mother says a prayer, then sings:

Star light, star bright,
First star I see tonight.
I wish I may,
I wish I might,
Have the wish I wish tonight.

As he nears the gate of slumber, he learns to pray – to speak his hopes into the night, hoping they'll move out the window, up over his home and neighborhood and beyond the universe into the ears of a higher deity. And he learns to wish – to gaze upon a twinkling star and convey his desires to relieve fears, provide help to someone in need or bring gifts.

As the Child begins to appreciate rhymes and poems, his Parents nurture him with longer songs that reinforce the dreamer's quest. They teach him a beloved classic from *Pinocchio*:

When you wish upon a star, makes no difference who you are.
Anything your heart desires will come to you.

If your heart is in your dreams, no request is too extreme.
When you wish upon a star as dreamers do,

Fate is kind, she brings to those who love
The sweet fulfillment of their secret longing.

Like a bolt out of the blue, fate steps in and sees you through.
When you wish upon a star, your dreams come true.

The Child learns early that an expressed wish will come to fruition if he wants it badly enough. But how? Has the Child not noticed someone within earshot who will hear his pleas and aim to please – perhaps a fairy godmother or singing cricket?

His Parents introduce other rhymes with important morals, like Dr. Seuss's *Oh, the Places You'll Go!*:

You have brains in your head.
You have feet in your shoes.
You can steer yourself
Any direction you choose.

The Child chuckles but dismisses these simple words. They do not resonate with the same easy magic of granted wishes.

The Child grows with life's joys, trials, setbacks and challenges – and hears they are part of "God's Will." Fortunes, fame, love or despair, it seems, are preordained. He believes it is his destiny to simply manifest what has already been decided for him.

THE TEEN AGE

Under the Parents' tutelage, the Child learns both discipline and to wish for the greater things in life. After all, there is always more – more gadgets, more places to see, more parties to attend and more sunrays to soak up. He most cherishes his playtime, relaxing time, do-nothing time – times that obscure and distract from the trials and tribulations of life.

Work is unpleasant; it has become a four-letter word. It is a necessity for his working class, and, he thinks, maybe a punishment for his ancestors' short-falls. And he brings this up when he wants sympathy. After all, he is not among those lucky enough to have wealth served up on a silver platter.

The Child begins to explore opportunities and experiences. Some seem fun, some hard and others not the least bit appealing. But he is zealous in his quest for discovery. He asks to try his hand at something of interest, something in-triguing and new, which requires thought and coordination. His Parents en-courage and excite him: "You can do anything you want in life." A noble statement, an encouraging phrase.

The Child's excitement is short-lived, however, as he soon learns that mas-tering the skill will require work. Maybe there's something else he'd enjoy more, something that's easier. The supportive Parents understand this was not meant to be, but the next opportunity will come, and maybe he'll commit to honing that new skill.

••••

"Every child is an artist. The problem is how to remain an artist once he grows up."

PABLO PICASSO
SPANISH PAINTER AND SCULPTOR

••••

Many sunsets elapse before the Child expresses his next subject of interest. The Parents note his eagerness and agree. Now, the Child begins to appreci-ate that every hobby comes at a price – both in time and money.

Each new interest and achievement means consistent practice, time away from friends and leisure, and sometimes even physical discomfort. He didn't foresee those investments.

More interests surface as the Child passes through adolescence, as do more lessons. The golden lesson? "A good deal." A deal where the price is low and the benefits are grand. When one gets a "good deal," he or she earns supreme bragging rights at a negligible cost. After all, no one wants to waste precious time and money on throwaway items – like helping someone and getting nothing in return. His goal is always to get the best deal.

His Parents begin providing an allowance – a noble gesture with no strings attached. Something for nothing? A good deal for sure. The Child begins to expect free money instead of appreciating the value of a gratuity.

As he begins to "hang out," peer pressure – to conform, to not standout, to be "normal" – rears its ugly head. Deviation from this societal pressure results in quick, pointed jabs. The pain is real – emotionally and often physically. Pain is also a four-letter word – another one to be avoided.

The Child wishes to be popular, to be famous, to be wanted, to be loved, which he believes will shield him from the storms of life. His Parents quarrel, bicker and fret over money. It is unsettling, awkward and painful. Pain must be avoided.

In his Life Sciences class, the Child admires the industriousness of ants and bees, which work incessantly. He marvels at their habits, yet knows we exterminate ants and fear bees. The Child learns of no human benefit offered by the ant and that the industrious bees produce honey and pollinate trees … for us. Good. We are consumers. We are takers.

In Government History class, he learns about people who worked, toiled, sacrificed and even died in the pursuit of a cause. The leaders almost always survived, but they too eventually went to their final resting places. Although he begins to develop an appreciation for their contributions, that is the past. He lives in the here and now, where the world should, in fact, revolve around him. He reads what the founding fathers wrote in the Declaration of Independence:

We hold these truths to be self-evident, that all men are created equal, that they are endowed by their Creator with certain unalienable Rights, that among these are Life, Liberty and the pursuit of Happiness.

All men created equal? The Child thinks not. He sees disparity and feels inequality; some have, some do not. These words do not resonate with truism. He pursues happiness in the company of peers and at parties. His view of the future is myopic.

••••

> ## "I pay the schoolmaster, but 'tis the schoolboys that educate my son."
> **RALPH WALDO EMERSON**
> AMERICAN PHILOSOPHER AND POET

••••

The Child witnesses many adults who are unhappy in their jobs, their marriages … their lives. Yet they tell him to go to school, get good grades and become a success, "just like them." The Child is puzzled over this dichotomy. Life begins to seem futile, direction and purpose elusive.

Liquor and drugs enter his life – conduits for mental bliss, a place where fears disappear and inhibitions are squelched. Maybe this is what life should be? His "uncool" Parents protest and punish, insisting he follow their lead, but he senses unrest and unhappiness in them and doesn't want to be like them. Defiance settles in. He admires and wants to be like the other teens, who convey the impression of independence from parental oppression. He learns the meaning of the old adage, "The enemy of my enemy is my friend." His circle of friends grows each time his Parents balk at the company he keeps. The decision to go along is easier than to stand on his own. His ego swells and must be protected, for he is subliminally broadcasting his perceived value to the world.

In adolescence, the Parents that were once revered and admired are now more like convenient resources that offer food, shelter and a springboard into the throngs of life. The Child has learned at an early age to "get," to expect to be cared for. The easy extraction of pleasure, and attaining the good life, are all that matter. The Parents, who once marveled at the sparkle in his eyes, are now lucky to get eye contact. Strangers begin to cohabitate in the Child's "space" – party animals, rappers, tough guys and television in general – an electronic attempt at telepathy, undermining the values the Child has learned from those who truly care about him.

At church, one doctrine stands out:

> *Ask, and it shall be given you; seek, and ye shall find;*
> *knock, and it shall be opened unto you.*

MATTHEW 7:7

And all things, whatsoever ye shall ask in prayer, believing, ye shall receive.
MATTHEW 21:22

In short, ask and you will receive! It is easy to ask, as easy as it is to wish. He sends more requests into the heavens, continues attending church and waits to "get." Giving to others is tantamount to being robbed; "getting" is the name of the game.

The Child's body matures in his teenage years and new senses take hold. The desire to be free and independent intensifies. His Parents are the first blockade to overcome. As adulthood fast approaches, he regards their care and guidance as unjust bondage that impairs his potential. He resents the responsibility they tell him he has to the family name. He never asked for, never wanted, those responsibilities; it seems unfair.

He goofs off in school and views teachers as authoritative figures who stymie his freedom. Filled with a restless spirit, he wants to hurry up, yet he does nothing. The Child fails to plan and therefore (unknowingly) plans to fail. He doesn't try, doesn't study and doesn't excel. He is not willing to help himself, and is slowly learning that the world will not help him in return.

••••

"None are so busy as those who do nothing."
FRENCH PROVERB

••••

With all elders, eye contact becomes elusive. His body language speaks volumes about his dissatisfaction, yet he only utters partial words, half sentences and slurred speech – a symbol of defiance.

The Child's wardrobe changes to mark his transition into the in-crowd. He expresses his burning desire to be different by dressing exactly like everyone else. Through their common bond – rejection of parents, elders, teachers and authority in general – groupies, cliques and gangs become like adopted families. The Child complains that there is nothing to do but stays out all night "getting it done."

••••

"Never forget that only dead fish
swim with the stream."
MALCOLM MUGGERIDGE
BRITISH JOURNALIST, AUTHOR AND SATIRIST

••••

Still, he somehow manages to squeak by and finish his senior year. High school graduation marks the end of adolescence and opens a symbolic gate into the future – a place where he will be an adult who no longer needs to listen to the counsel of Parents or obey the presumed commands of old-fashioned dictators who are out of tune with the world.

On graduation day, he dresses in his best clothes, wondering why his Father has spent so much time polishing his shoes and why his Mother won't stop straightening his hair. As they approach the arena, the traffic becomes heavy, and the Child momentarily wonders why so many cars are present, but his mind is primarily distracted by the thought of the parties that await him tonight.

He finds his rightful place among the students – all dressed alike in their gowns and caps with tassels. The band begins to play, and the students are given the go-ahead to march in unison toward the center of the arena. As he walks, he is amazed to see what seems to be thousands of people standing in the periphery, clapping as the student ensemble forges forward. The whistles, claps and cheers fill the air with excitement. The flicker of hundreds of flashes from eager photographers creates a milieu of stardom. Though still cynical about all the hullabaloo, the Child can't help but feel a little pride – and even a pinch of arrogance; he is in a place where many others are not. His "real life" is about to begin.

The Child listens to the many presenters – students, school officials and guest speakers. They speak of the transition this day marks – the passage into a new world of opportunities. The speeches seem endless (and mostly meaningless) to the Child, whose mind is still focused on what comes next, but the valedictorian gets through to him – if only for a brief moment – when she quotes Walt Disney: *All our dreams can come true ... if we have the courage to pursue them.*

With the flick of a tassel and the throw of a cap, the Child crosses the symbolic threshold into a world where he is free to make decisions and blaze new trails. The now-independent Child has the power to choose. He believes he will soon be invincible.

DECISIONS

What will the Child do with this newfound power? What road will he take? His Parents reluctantly offer a symbolic release from their "bondage." He can now make his own decisions. He may even be encouraged to leave the nest soon. Life will become his new teacher. The Child is his own master.

He looks at his own standing, his environment and the pursuits of others – and the grass is definitely greener on the other side, or so he thinks.

••••

"The circumstances of others seem good to us, while ours seem good to others."

PUBLILIUS SYRUS
FORMER SLAVE AND LATIN WRITER

••••

Confused and without ambition, he begins to take life's challenges more personally. Choosing the "right" and easiest road has implications – financial and time costs. Resources and tolerance from his Parents are now limited, and play is curtailed.

The Child wishes for a breakthrough, some divine intervention. Decisions are hard. Consequences are real. Repercussions are possible. He could ease the mental turbulence by winning the lottery – a cheap risk with monumental rewards. He plays. He doesn't win.

He ponders his choices and concludes there are four options:
- College
- P&L (Party and Leach)
- P&L (Profit & Loss) with a business of his own
- Job

••••

"Through indecision, opportunity is often lost."

LATIN PROVERB

••••

The future is everything. The right (and easiest) path must exist, but in the absence of all the facts, no decision is a decision in itself. Time is his most precious commodity – time to relax, to party and to kill time – yet he whines of boredom and a litany of other woes. With no purpose, he drifts like a ship without a rudder.

••••

"Nothing is more difficult, and therefore more precious, than to be able to decide."

NAPOLEON BONAPARTE
FRENCH EMPEROR AND MILITARY LEADER

••••

In the midst of this pursuit of time, the Child senses that the world is defining him. His Parents, neighbors, friends and teachers have offered direction and advice from their perceived perches of servitude. He waits for the invisible verdict to wrestle through the discourse and make itself known. He no longer feels in control but doesn't yet see the possibility of actually taking the reins and defining himself to the world.

The music of "seem-to-have-it-all" artists permeates his environment, providing an escape and instant gratification. Lyrics imbued with obscenities, hatred, racism, sexism and disgust begin to temper the Child's psyche, and what's left of his uniqueness further dissipates. The songs describe bold actions; subversive innuendos cleverly disguised in moving or catchy musical rhythms engrain themselves into his subconscious. The Child doesn't yet realize that some people know very little, but they know it fluently.

••••

"Anger is a bad counselor."

FRENCH PROVERB

••••

Video games and movies also offer a welcome distraction – a way to immerse himself in a make-believe world where current trials can be forgotten. He particularly likes action heroes. There is something magical about their prowess, tenacity and ability to eliminate the offending bad guy (and other troubles) and survive. The psychology of elimination embeds itself into his psyche, and, unbeknownst to him, he begins to act out the repressed feelings. Unconsciously, but with the accuracy of a masterful surgeon, he begins to dissect his world, separating people into two categories: "fun and laid-back" and "know-nothings" – namely inconveniences, dictators with menial requests that serve no purpose but to consume his time and energy. The images he receives shape the ones he transmits. Feelings of hatred, disgust and inadequacy emerge. Insecurity takes root.

In a furtive fashion, the Child begins to tell others to die – or at least disappear. His anger, confusion, misunderstandings and arguments start to erode relationships. If only they were out of his way he could live his own life.

The Child learns instead to kill time, to murder opportunity. That he can control, and that accomplishment satisfies his psyche. No one can tell him what to do anymore.

••••

"All the treasures of earth
cannot bring back one lost moment."
FRENCH PROVERB

••••

The Child's speech is marked with "filler" words like "cool," "sweet," "um" and "whatever" – words that fill the space and continuum of free speech but really carry no substance, no conviction, no follow-through and no call to action. Defiant, rebellious and determined not to listen to reason, he refuses to do chores, or shows halfhearted attempts to acquiesce "nagging" parents. His Parents turn on the tough love. Contradictory and painful bickering ensues without clear winners and losers, disrupting family harmony.

The Child feels he needs some luck – to find that "gravy train" he knows exists but doesn't know how to find. Pretense intensifies in his social circle – from his casual walk to his carefree attitude. Yet, in his state of funk, going along feels like mediocrity. In reality, where he is going in life is a question of mind over matter, and since he doesn't mind, it doesn't matter. Ironically, success can often be measured more truthfully by internal rather than external criteria.

The Parents, filled with anguish, step back and let the Child mess up his own life. Where did his charms go? His intrinsic power and potential?

The Child, who wonders where his kindred spirits are, is impulsive and, like so many, a **Wisher** ...

· · · ·

wish (n):

1. A desire, longing or strong inclination for a specific thing. **2.** An expression of a desire, longing or strong inclination; a petition. **3.** Something desired or longed for.

wish (v):

To have or feel a desire.

Source: *American Heritage Dictionary of the English Language, Fourth Edition, 2000*

WORK

Opportunity strikes, and the Child receives a job offer. The gods are finally listening! He begins to work, excited about discovering his new potential. He learns to be productive in the service of others, in return for remuneration.

••••

"Circumstances! I make circumstances!"

NAPOLEON BONAPARTE
FRENCH EMPEROR AND MILITARY LEADER

••••

First paycheck in hand, he realizes how different – and special – earned money feels. He will spend it more wisely than past allowances, he decides. He excitedly opens the envelope … and learns firsthand that the government gets first dibs on his earnings. He had heard of such a thing, but it never concerned him, because it never applied to him. Now it does. He gripes to no avail.

The money is good for now, so he splurges. Days and weeks unfold, and his cash doesn't seem to go far enough. His job becomes monotonous, and the Child begins to ponder other opportunities. In the meantime, he learns to keep a schedule, follow directions and tend to customer needs – responsibilities he had never before fully grasped. As routine settles in, so does disappointment.

The Child works hard but still cannot afford the things he *wants*. So he borrows money to buy his first mode of transportation. More than just a vehicle, this purchase is a ticket to enlarged social circles and new liberties and explorations. And the car, he believes, is an obvious prerequisite for getting girls.

Though his Father had often talked about the day he would help his son purchase his first car and had warned him about the dangers of spending large sums of money without first doing the research or understanding the lay of the land, the Child doesn't want his Father cramping his style, or encroaching on his manhood by hogging the spotlight on his big day. He takes a buddy along instead.

The car he has been watching for a while – drooling over, in fact, during his daily commute to and from work – is still sitting there, beckoning him to take its powerful, turbocharged, 8-cylinder engine for a test drive. The shiny red paint, polished chrome, mag wheels and supersized racing tires rumble in harmony with the finely tuned motor and boisterous escape of hot gases through the exhaust system. The leather interior spells comfort and luxury.

He senses the power that accelerator will give him, thinking that this purchase will set him apart from all. Even though anyone can "press the pedal to the metal," owning this powerful car is his right, his strength, his persona. *This* is his car; no other will do. It is his first major decision without his Father's input, and he doesn't want advice. He doesn't think about consequences like expensive insurance premiums on a muscle car, the cost of specialty tires or gasoline expenditures.

The Child imagines the envy in his friends' eyes, and how impressed the girls will be when they see him in this manly vehicle. His furrowed brow, clammy palms, increased heart rate and accelerated breathing all indicate he is about to make a decision. The experienced car salesman sees the eager lad and, from all the way across the lot, knows the car is already sold – at sticker price. After all, the Child is practically drooling on its hood. He won't haggle. And he doesn't. Sold!

The Child agrees to repay his lender, but in time he comes to realize that many of his promises are empty carriages of wishful intentions. Instead, new expenses take priority over making his monthly payments. The fancy car has brought a plentitude of beautiful dates, which has placed him in the "hip" crowd. This status requires perpetual party attendance, going out, driving around friends and the like – all of which quickly consume his money and time. Creditors must take a backseat to more important social needs.

The Child doesn't yet understand that his word, like the car he purchased, has value attached to it, and that his word and reputation are beginning to lose precious value in the marketplace. Through his choices, he is unwillingly and subliminally communicating his priorities, plus his self-worth, to the world.

The Child starts to slack off at work, often showing up late – or not at all. After all, they're lucky to have him there in the first place, and he has better things to do – or so he thinks. But the business owner needs consistent workers with positive attitudes – attributes that are now waning from the Child's performance. Not careful what he wishes for, he gets it; he doesn't have a job to hate anymore.

••••

"Labor disgraces no man; unfortunately you occasionally find men disgrace labor."

ULYSSES S. GRANT
18TH PRESIDENT OF THE UNITED STATES

••••

A few days without work responsibilities appear to be a godsend. But with more time to party, he soon discovers that the "party animals" expect contributions to the standard supply of beer, liquor or smokes. Realizing his friends can carry him for only so long, he knows another job is inevitable.

••••

"As a teenager I was so insecure. I was the type of guy that never fitted in because he never dared to choose. I was convinced I had absolutely no talent at all. For nothing. And that thought took away all my ambition too."

JOHNNY DEPP
AMERICAN ACTOR AND MUSICIAN

••••

Now a practiced master at killing time and murdering opportunity, he hones those skills. Insecurity and apprehension permeate the air. His extended family and friends give good-natured advice about what he "cannot" or "should not" do, largely a reflection of their own experiences, casually laying figments of inferiority, inadequacy, guilt, rejection and unworthiness in his psyche. He is unaware that some will kick a good man while he is down to make *them* feel strong. By having these seeds implanted in his fertile mind, he reaps ample weeds instead of grand deeds.

The Child comes face-to-face with one of life's great conundrums – reciprocity. The value he places on himself, the world returns in kind. When he thinks small, he gets small. So he must think big to win big, but securing a higher position seems daunting and elusive.

The Child scours help-wanted ads and makes a few well-chosen personal pleas to local merchants – to no avail. Weeks go by before another opportunity presents itself. He accepts the job and commits to becoming more responsible.

And he follows through, working hard to build a nice little nest egg, accruing some new social skills along the way. The Child considers college but decides to forgo an education. He needs funds for dates, so he must make money quickly. Though he has no home to speak of, no savings and no plans for the future, he springs for fancier accessories and gadgets for his dream car – thoroughly satisfying his ego. He has learned to work but not to aspire.

••••

"Tell me thy company and I will tell thee what thou art."

MIGUEL DE CERVANTES
SPANISH NOVELIST AND POET

••••

Old friends return to his life and soon he has plenty of new friends as well – friends who want his company *and* free transportation. Satisfied that people need him, he complies. Soon the car becomes a transport mechanism not only for his friends but also for spent cigarette ashes, discarded beer bottles and leftover meals. Feeling used, the Child realizes he must change his life; he must find a new job in a new location to begin a new pursuit.

••••

"Whatever is good to know is difficult to learn."

GREEK PROVERB

••••

He wants respect – demands it, in fact. But he hasn't realized the difference between demanding respect and *commanding* it. This philosophical difference affects his subconscious actions – and keeps him from getting what he wants. By communicating to others that he doesn't respect *them*, he communicates that he is not worthy of respect.

The Child is never alone, yet he feels lonely all the time. He squelches the emptiness with another beer, another shot, another smoke – mistakenly thinking it puts him in control. He falls in line – much drinking, little thinking.

Desperately needing external stimuli for energy and direction, the Child ironically states, "Life sucks." Yet his *lifestyle* is what sucks – draining his energy and life. He has not learned to give or to create. He is a late bloomer.

••••

> "There is no use whatever trying to
> help people who do not help themselves.
> You cannot push anyone up a ladder
> unless he be willing to climb himself."
>
> **ANDREW CARNEGIE**
> SCOTTISH-AMERICAN INDUSTRIALIST
> AND BUSINESSMAN

••••

A faint trace of a plan for success emerges – perceptible but still out of reach. His quest for success is superficial for now, not yet fully ingrained, energized and activated. He continues to traverse the stagnating swamps of idle motivation where "*wannabes*" abound but "*gonnabes*" are scarce.

He works, waiting to get that paycheck, that raise. Inflation and emergency vehicle repairs dissipate his earnings. Angry and resentful, he becomes a pessimist with a difficulty for every solution. He feels lame, with plenty of people to blame.

••••

> "Those who despise money will
> eventually sponge on their friends."
>
> **CHINESE PROVERB**

••••

His friends laugh at his job and efforts, which have so far yielded little money and little progress. "Why do you work so hard?" they ask. "We are here, just enjoying life. Come with us. Have a beer. Be cool."

Having drifted through life waiting for the Lord's will to manifest itself or for dumb luck to strike, instead of blazing the trail with his own skill, the Child has allowed failure to become his sole claim to fame. He complains deftly about the bad luck he seems destined to attract, soliciting sympathy from any receptive ear and "stealing" unearned energy from willing souls to maintain his façade. The world is out to get him, he tells himself, and everyone who's offered a "poor you" sees it too.

One day he comes across a poem by Dale Wimbrow:

The Man in the Glass

When you get what you want in your struggle for self
And the world makes you king for a day,
Just go to the mirror and look at yourself
And see what that man has to say.

For it isn't your father or mother or wife
Whose judgment upon you must pass.
The fellow whose verdict counts most in your life
Is the one staring back from the glass.

Some may think you're a straight-shooting chum,
And think you a wonderful guy.
But the man in the glass says you're only a bum
If you can't look him straight in the eye.

He's the fellow to please – never mind all the rest,
For he's with you clear to the end.
And you've passed your most dangerous and difficult test
If the man in the glass is your friend.

You may fool the whole world down the pathway of years
And get pats on the back as you pass.
But your final reward will be heartache and tears
If you've cheated the man in the glass.

The wisdom seems practical, but he does not yet understand the significance for *him*. He wants to feel proud, but for what? He becomes a professional spectator of Olympic athletes, businessmen, architects, lawyers and young inventors who accrue gold medals and awards. If only he could have been so lucky. His excuses communicate why he is not among their ranks.

The Child has heard that one is born either a leader or a follower. Failing to recognize that what is in his mind, heart and soul could make him a great leader, he resigns himself to his "destiny"; fate has clearly made him a follower.

••••

"A lazy person, whatever the talents
with which he starts out, has condemned
himself to second-rate thoughts,
and to second-rate friends."

CYRIL VERNON CONNOLLY
ENGLISH INTELLECTUAL,
LITERARY CRITIC AND WRITER

••••

With a laissez-faire attitude toward acquiring skills, wisdom and know-how, he hopes to become a success by osmosis, by rubbing shoulders with someone important, successful and influential. This is easy, but success still seems just as distant. He continues to believe, however, that when the time is right, he will spring forward – a new champion with the complete skill set to make a killing. He doesn't yet understand the value of *doing*.

••••

"Each man makes
his own shipwreck."

LATIN PROVERB

••••

Still steering a boat with no rudder, he drifts aimlessly to and fro as the wind, currents and life circumstances dictate. The Child has a foundation – innate attributes as well as talents picked up along the way – but he dismisses the edge that has been given to him. His glass is half empty, and he doesn't understand that to fill it, he need only change his perspective. Experience is an effective teacher, as it provides *personal* instruction – but at a high price.

The Child doesn't comprehend that both success and failure are largely the result of habits. As the years progress, many dead-end jobs fill his résumé. He has not yet learned that commitment, sacrifice, persistence and tenacity must be nurtured from within. He has instead mastered the art of being *wishy-washy*. Like a rocking horse, he exhibits lots of motion but is going nowhere.

••••

wish-y-wash-y (adj.):
Lacking in strength of character or purpose; ineffective.

Source: American Heritage Dictionary of the English Language, Fourth Edition, 2000

ATTRACTION

The company of many girls has brought laughter, heartache, amusement and disappointment to the Child over the years. But, a closet romantic, he presses on, still seeking the beautiful, smart, playful girl of his dreams.

One day, while visiting his Mother's shop, he spots a girl unlike any other he has met. Relatively short in stature, with long hair, she accentuates her feminine form with a quirky, vividly colored dress. As she peruses the store in her petite high heels, she mesmerizes him with the confident yet humble sway of her stride and the flow of her dress. Though he tries to pretend he's not staring at her, their glances occasionally meet, and her endearing eyes silently summon him, offering only a millisecond of relief from her trance when those gentle eyelashes obscure her power. He is smitten.

••••

"Love makes your soul
crawl out from its hiding place."
ZORA NEALE HURSTON
AMERICAN FOLKLORIST AND AUTHOR

••••

He learns that this girl is a regular customer and begs his Mother for an introduction. She eagerly obliges with a knowing smile that would ordinarily embarrass him, but today, nothing matters except meeting this girl.

He musters up his most respectable self and reaches out to shake her hand. As her manicured fingers stretch to meet his, a million thoughts traverse his mind. He visually savors the delicate nature of her forearm and, when their hands connect, the softness of her skin and firmness of her touch – a welcome contrast to his physical strength. He manages one clear thought, despite his racing mind: This young lady is special, and she must not get away. Small talk ensues – though he is more focused on her moving lips and melodious tone than her words. While he tries to break the spell long enough to ask her for a date, she interrupts, advising that errands must be finished.

The imminence of her departure stirs his courage. As he gestures for her to hold for a minute while he thinks up a winning invitation, his unsteady hand knocks a jar of coffee beans onto the floor. Mortified (this was not the attention-getting strategy he had in mind), he apologizes profusely and asks that she be careful not to cut herself on the broken glass. She giggles at his awkwardness and his concern. The spill has given him the extra seconds, and the desperation, that he needed to make his request. "Ummm," he stammers. "Would you like to go to dinner with me tonight around seven – to allow me to make up for my clumsiness?"

She considers. While she would not ordinarily accept an invitation from a stranger, she knows his Mother, he seems nice and she has some time available. As she agrees, her gleaming smile leaves the Child in such a vivacious stupor that it takes several moments before he is clearheaded enough to answer his Mother's excited questions.

The Child and young lady begin to date. The attraction seems mutually electrifying, and his thoughts all turn to her. His energy levels intensify, and his nervous and befuddled brain distorts many of his "let me impress you" introductory prose statements, earning him more than one unintended laugh from the object of his affection. Fortunately, a mutual magnetic attraction is palpable.

This young lady finds the Child's "weirdness" intriguing and endearing. She shares many of his hobbies – adventure video games, museums, strolls on the beach and Rollerblading in the park. He shares thoughts, experiences and aspirations unlike any she has heard before, communicating hints of a man who desires success and to be in control of his destiny. But he also displays a degree of humility unlike any of her former suitors. It's not "look what I did," but rather, "look what I dream." And instead of gossip or the standard recital of sports scores and trivia that she has become accustomed to from most of her former dates, he wants to hear *her* thoughts and vision for the future as well.

He smiles when he notices her occasionally steal furtive glances of admiration at his physique. She relishes in the comfort that his warm embrace provides when she's had a long day, and dramatizes it a bit during scary movies, knowing her fear will invite his arms to encircle her. And he remains mesmerized by her intellect, her thirst for travel and new experiences and the way she can talk with such zeal about a book that she makes him want to read it too, so he can be on the same page. Her lively, enticing laugh, caring heart, entrancing grace and harmonious disposition leave him craving more – more of her mind, her embrace and even her mere presence in the room.

Weeks elapse, and the Child finds himself conversing about topics, people and places he has thus far never explored or even considered. Companionship and friendship become intertwined in a magical, chemical potion. He has fallen in love.

In her company, days become hours, hours pass like minutes and minutes tick away as fast as seconds. Shared joys become double joys, and shared sorrows only half sorrows.

Finally, the Child knows what he wants – marriage, a successful job so he can be a good provider for his family, a fine home and to make a difference in the lives of others. His Beloved has made him think in unselfish – and unfamiliar – ways. The prospect of sharing his life with her has reinvigorated and excited him, and he knows it means responsibility, consistency and the opportunity to build a joint life in the pursuit of happiness – a life beyond himself and his personal needs. He begins to see how giving to another human being can be a loving expression of self with magnificent rewards.

But how does he get to this place – especially when cash is in such short supply? For a fleeting moment the Child considers how sweet it would be to marry into a wealthy family and accrue the silver platter he'd been deprived of at birth – only to realize that his Beloved comes from a working-class family too. One more wish not granted.

••••

> "Shallow men believe in luck.
> Strong men believe in cause and effect."
> **RALPH WALDO EMERSON**
> AMERICAN PHILOSOPHER AND POET

••••

If only "the gods" would tell him what to do – and how and when to do it. He does not yet fully understand that life, as he wants it to be, must be *created* – and that it is within his power to do so. He has the wherewithal to make a difference, yet he wonders what difference he will make.

His inner voice seems to respond, but only in whispers, and the Child cannot yet discern the message or the direction. Until now, life's glory and purpose have not revealed themselves. But he is now acutely aware that his countless efforts to kill time have proven pointless and ethereal, producing no long-lasting substance or progress, only wasting time and money he'll never get back.

• • • •

"You must have control of the authorship
of your own destiny. The pen that writes your
life story must be held by your own hand."
DR. IRENE C. KASSORLA
AUSTRALIAN PSYCHOLOGIST

• • • •

"No more," he says. He begins to feel the spark igniting – a burning desire to succeed, to share, to live! Despite the restlessness still churning in his psyche, a barely audible inner voice seems to be calling for action, a new strategy that will yield *lasting* value. He senses some impending transformation – unsettling, yet powerful. He remembers watching a baby bird leave the nest, taking its first leap into the wild blue yonder. Scared to let go, the bird clung for dear life to the nest – and then it let go, full of confidence, as though it knew all along that it could do this. Despite the wind's resistance against the resolute bird's wings, it took flight and soared. The Child feels a connection to the bird and to the world.

• • • •

"We have two ears and one mouth
that we may listen more and talk less."
GREEK PROVERB

• • • •

The Child seeks mentors – seasoned individuals who have trodden the paths he feels he must now traverse. Now he wants to listen rather than speak, to absorb their teachings instead of assuming he knows it all, to request their guidance instead of trying to soak up their prowess through passive osmosis.

His Beloved's family welcomes him into the fold, and his support system grows exponentially. Without solicitation, these "strangers" suddenly care about his existence, his dreams and his challenges. He begins to see the value of giving unselfishly to others – no tangible returns, compensation or parity expected, and yet the personal rewards of satisfaction run deep. Happiness, he learns, can be found in the service of others.

Recognizing that he is special to their younger sister, his Beloved's older brothers share wonderful stories and insights that shed light on new possibilities and paths the Child has never been exposed to or even considered. One of them recommends that he check out some business books and directs him to the family library, where he discovers John C. Maxwell's *Talent Is Never Enough*. He is inspired to learn that:

· More than 50 percent of all Fortune 500 CEOs had C or C-minus averages in college.
· Sixty-five percent of all U.S. senators (and presidents) ranked in the bottom half of their classes.
· More than 50 percent of millionaire entrepreneurs never finished college!

He gets it now: It starts with him. He has lost some time, but he can recover. Privacy, solace and quietude become precious as he learns to delve into the subconscious and decipher the mystical messages hiding within. He changes his style of dress to mirror his aspired heights. He begins to stand tall, walk with a bold stride and look strangers in the eye as he greets them – often for no reason other than to bid good tidings. He is resolute. His self-esteem increases, and he exudes confidence.

••••

"Be a Columbus to whole new continents and worlds within you, opening new channels, not of trade, but of thought."
HENRY DAVID THOREAU
AMERICAN AUTHOR, POET AND NATURALIST

••••

His Beloved's father, a scientist with a charismatic, absent-minded-professor look about him, never misses an opportunity to share his marvels at even the tiniest elements of life – and his enthusiasm is contagious. The Child becomes aware that everything on Earth, and in the universe, is energy at the atomic level – an intangible form of energy that initiated every one of the billions of individual cells in his body and every atom of matter. All substances give the illusion of permanence but are, in fact, only representations of varying states of energy. He ponders the DNA structure of all living things and how it harbors an infinite source of information, a world of potential. Can *he* tap into this infinite resource and change the world?

He finds that his happiness increases as he makes others happier. He has been looking at individuals he admires, wanting what they have, but not *seeing* what makes them successful. Doctors, firemen, police officers, scientists, carpenters, teachers, homemakers and grocery clerks – all help many, many people. Their satisfaction seems to come from a job well done and the value they bring to the lives of others. Life is not, as he once thought, a race to be the first to cross the finish line and get the grand prize all for himself.

The Child begins to help out more at home, with his Beloved's family and in the neighborhood. Others' gratitude is all the reward he needs. It fuels his confidence, happiness and sense of purpose and connectedness to the universe.

His desire for the *easy life* becomes his need to **make a life**. The Child will become an agent of change – for himself and others.

EVERYBODY WISHES, BUT FEW ARE *DOERS*

The Child, who has always wished upon stars and then lamented his unfulfilled desires, begins to reexamine this method. He hears people around him wishing for things they would like to see happen, things they are going to do someday and things that should go their way. He sees that the moment these desires are uttered, the Wishers, or the so-called "talkers," enjoy temporary satisfaction and relative peace of mind, feeling that the world has now been notified of their worth and that their requests are now theirs for the taking. Yet they fail to take action to make those wishes into reality.

••••

"Great minds have purposes,
others have wishes."

WASHINGTON IRVING
AMERICAN AUTHOR, ESSAYIST, BIOGRAPHER AND HISTORIAN

••••

As the Child mentally revisits his own experiences with wishing, he realizes that these words were, more often than not, a verbal and mental sedative providing a false sense of impending achievement. In reality, countless wishes failed to materialize. He begins to understand the bridge between rhetoric and reality: action.

Suddenly the Child remembers a poster he once saw at a shopping mall – and immediately discounted as "cheesy." It read:

*Happy are those who dream dreams,
and are ready to pay the price to make them come true.*

••••

"Genius is 1 percent inspiration
and 99 percent perspiration!"

THOMAS EDISON
AMERICAN INVENTOR, SCIENTIST AND BUSINESSMAN

••••

The Child takes this to heart and commits to change his habits as well as his psyche, motivation and commitment. He vows to speak and act with conviction, knowing full well that he will have to pay the price – whether it be money, leisure time or sacrificing old habits. He doesn't yet understand the full significance of this revelation, only that something needs to change.

And the world responds. New windows of opportunity open, despite his slow start. A note in a church bulletin stirs his consciousness:

Do not despise small beginnings.
Every giant redwood started out as a little seed.
Every skyscraper began with a shovel of dirt digging down to go up!
Every eagle hatched from an egg, and every butterfly from a cocoon.
Every best-selling book and blockbuster film started as a thought.
Every grand invention began as a little idea.
Every good marriage started with a glance and a smile.
Every great hero used to be a little baby.
Every world-record musky started as a tiny fish egg!
Every heart-stirring song began with a single note.
So – the world of small seeds, little ideas,
single notes and fish eggs is the place where true greatness is born!

Do not despise small beginnings –
they contain the magic of wonderful hopes yet unfilled.

Wishing for success and committing to it, he realizes, are two very different things with very different energy levels. A wish is a passive utterance, a hope or expectation that someone or something else will make it happen. To commit, however, means tapping into an inner energy source that, when properly articulated and acted upon, has the power to drive us and to alert the world that we are on a mission.

••••

"I don't think much of a man who is
not wiser today than he was yesterday."

ABRAHAM LINCOLN
16TH PRESIDENT OF THE U.S.

••••

The Child has a profound realization that the best investment he can make is in himself and that by employing the three P's (Persistence, Perspiration and Passion), he can, in fact, make his dreams come true. The power has been within him all along – clouded and suppressed. It needs awakening. He concludes that the way to get ahead, and stay ahead, is to use his head.

He sets time aside for discussion and reading. His movie and musical interests change to more positive influences. He reads and watches biographies of individuals who exude the values he is now beginning to value. He treasures his solitary time – peaceful meditative time in which he can contemplate and formulate action plans.

••••

"Mentoring is a brain to pick,
an ear to listen,
and a push in the right direction."
JOHN CROSBY
AMERICAN POLITICIAN

••••

He needs training and guidance. He decides to learn how to tap into his very own mental state and condition his thought processes to be independent, strong, tenacious and committed. The Child seeks more mentors whose experience he can leverage – wise and trusted counselors who have learned to overcome the fears that trick us into holding back our potential while subconsciously persuading us that we're "saving" ourselves. These confidants will help him establish direction and nurture his burning desire to reach his aspirations. He is teachable!

A sense of urgency manifests itself, for he has come to understand that time and tide wait for no man. No one has ever seen tomorrow, but the Child can feel possibilities brewing for his future.

••••

"If you hear a voice within you say,
'You cannot paint,' then by all means paint
and that voice will be silenced."
VINCENT VAN GOGH
DUTCH POSTIMPRESSIONIST PAINTER

••••

The Child focuses his attention on his future career. This time, he will pursue opportunities with laser-sharp concentration and diligence, discounting all other work options, for his energy must be applied in the direction of his dreams. He does his research and focuses his job search on finding *the* opportunity – one that will allow him to build a *career* – rather than pursuing the many opportunities that come along just to have a *job*. Many rejections come his way in this process, but they do not temper his tenacity; he knows that he is just a few no's away from a yes.

His perspective on work has changed, and he now goes into interviews knowing that he has value to offer potential employers, and that they do not *owe* him anything, nor should they automatically be grateful for his interest in working for them. In the past, his lackadaisical attitude toward job searching – blundered interviews, misspellings on his résumé, missed appointments, unfriendly disposition to receptionists, cocky manner, desperation, lack of qualifications and experience, inopportune timing and sub-optimum dress – has resulted in many, many rejections. Today, however, he knows that success comes when preparedness meets opportunity, so he makes an effort to impress, to convey his enthusiasm, intelligence and worth to potential employers.

It pays off – with an offer from his first-choice company and a starting salary beyond his comprehension. Vowing to treat this job as an opportunity rather than a means to a paycheck, he gets to work early and stays late. He studies, makes inquiries, offers ideas, asks to participate in group meetings, meets his commitments and does his work to the best of his ability. While his best may not always meet his Boss's best expectations, the Child takes constructive criticism well and willingly redoes the work, using what he learns along the way to do a better job on future tasks.

His Boss knows that a person can be taught anything, but that attitude comes from within. And while the Child is still learning his trade, his attitude – his commitment to the task and loyalty to the company – is his greatest asset.

In time, the Boss knows, the Child will become a leader and will make *him* look good. So he takes the Child under his wing, becoming an unofficial mentor, showing him the ropes and sharing pearls of wisdom not found in any book or taught in any school – lessons one learns only on the job and from life. For instance, the Boss asks him how much money he has saved. The Child feels uncomfortable with this question, as he only has a meager savings to speak of, so he utters a ho-hum answer. The Boss tells him that he needs at least three months' salary in savings so he will have the confidence he needs to make long-term decisions, not just immediate ones. To illustrate this point, the Boss explains that if he ever needs to make a difficult decision at work, he will not have to worry about being fired if the risk doesn't pay off. With a safety net in place, he will be more willing to make tough choices on behalf of the company, which will, in the long run, most likely be the right decisions. He must be able to put himself on the line with his convictions.

••••

"By three methods we may learn wisdom:
First, by reflection, which is noblest;
second, by imitation, which is easiest; and third,
by experience, which is the bitterest."
CONFUCIUS
CHINESE THINKER AND EDUCATOR

••••

The Child works hard and gains more and more respect, eventually earning a leadership position over a team. He feels that he is the "greatest thing since sliced bread." His Boss continues to regularly stop by his office to chat about life and impart even more leadership lessons. For example, he tells the Child that if he ever catches him yelling at, berating or denigrating an employee, he will be fired immediately. The perplexed Child quickly retraces his actions; he thankfully has not raised his voice or chastised anyone. The Boss explains that an employee has limited power compared to him and, in some cases, may even vent; they have limited recourse and need an outlet. Bosses who return acrimonious dialogue with people who do not have this power, stature or position are abusing their authority! It is also a sign of insecurity. Those lost in their own myths can cut a fine figure but generally make poor human beings. Team synergy, building people up and mutual respect are paramount in an organization. The Child is inspired by his Boss's direction; he will imitate this mentor.

The Child is to contribute. He offers many stellar ideas to the company – including improved inspection methods, more thorough procedures, more efficient manufacturing techniques and moral-building exercises. Many of these contributions earn him recognition, plaques and rewards, yet others get relegated to the back burner or even discarded. His Boss, careful not to dampen the Child's enthusiasm, explains that some ideas were not meant to be, while others just need time to germinate and be understood. If he continues to offer better and better ideas, he will soon be the one making the decisions about which paths to follow.

The Child's professional network grows steadily as he makes new contacts on the job and expands his social circles. He befriends a neighbor who works for a national radio program and has access to many quality books. Having learned of the Child's love for reading, the man rummages through the multitude of books sent in for review and selects a chosen few. That evening, he approaches the Child with a gift, one far better than the gadgets and gizmos he once hoped for upon receiving a present – a heavy box of enlightenment and hard-earned wisdom, books that can give the Child an edge and expand his horizons.

••••

"A capacity and taste for reading gives access to whatever has been discovered by others. It is the key, or one of the keys, to the already solved problems. And not only so; it gives relish and facility for successfully pursuing the unsolved ones."

ABRAHAM LINCOLN
16TH PRESIDENT OF THE U.S.

••••

That night, he dives into the book that catches his attention first – *Sequoia-Size Success: Unlocking Your Potential for Greatness*. Paul Tsika explains that many people who are drowning in life's problems are actually being weighed down, not by their experiences but by their lack of vision. A big vision will help overcome any problem, but a small vision or no vision at all will allow the smallest of problems to take us off course. His secret to overcoming adversity? We must:

· Foresee our afflictions constructively
· Focus our attention correctly

· Finish our assignments completely
· Form our attitudes correctly, and
· Face our adversaries confidently.

In Brian Souza's *Become Who You Were Born to Be*, the Child reads that unsuccessful people do what's easiest in the short run instead of what's right in the long run. They are controlled by moods, not by values. They provide excuses in lieu of solutions. When challenged, they are more apt to quit than to persevere. They rely on external, not internal, motivation. And when they speak, their actions frequently differ from their words.

He vows to embody Stephen R. Covey's *7 Habits of Highly Effective People*:

· Be proactive
· Begin with the end in mind
· Put first things first
· Think "win-win"
· Seek first to understand – then to be understood
· Synergize
· Sharpen the saw

Daniel Coyle's *The Talent Code* describes the simple laws of learning that have inspired world-class conductors, musicians and athletes with very humble beginnings:

· Explanation
· Demonstration
· Imitation
· Correction
· Repetition

Commitment, Coyle explains, is also key, citing a 1997 study by Gary McPherson. His research found that progress and potential in students taking music lessons could be best predicted not by any measurable aptitude or trait, but by a tiny, powerful idea the children had *before* beginning training – that they were in it for the long haul. And the results were staggering. With the same amount of practice, the long-term-commitment group outperformed the short-term-commitment group by 400 percent! What's more, with a mere 20 minutes of weekly practice, the long-termers progressed faster than short-termers who practiced for an hour and a half.

••••

"Don't look for the high, quick improvement.
Seek the small improvement one day at a time."
JOHN WOODEN
COACH WHO LED UCLA BASKETBALL TEAM TO NINE CHAMPIONSHIPS

••••

This reminds the Child of a book he once began and liked, but never finished. He resurrects his copy of *Talent Is Never Enough*, in which he reads that the world is full of talented people who do not reach the pinnacles of success. They practice and perform their skills on a daily basis but lack some key ingredients. He commits to memory the 13 key choices to maximize his talent:

- Belief lifts his talent
- Passion energizes his talent
- Initiative activates his talent
- Focus directs his talent
- Preparation positions his talent
- Practice sharpens his talent
- Perseverance sustains his talent
- Courage tests his talent
- Teachability expands his talent
- Character protects his talent
- Relationships influence his talent
- Responsibility strengthens his talent
- Teamwork multiplies his talent

• • • •

"Talent is cheaper than table salt.
What separates the talented individual from
the successful one is a lot of hard work."

STEPHEN KING
AMERICAN AUTHOR OF CONTEMPORARY HORROR,
SUSPENSE, SCIENCE FICTION AND FANTASY FICTION

• • • •

He begins to understand that talent alone is not enough. The world is full of talented individuals who have not fulfilled their true potential, who are waiting on the sidelines for life to call them into the game. Why? It is their decisions, attitudes, commitments, selfishness, impatience, effort levels, failure to adapt and lack of social skills that hinder their progress. Success also hinges on the choices we make. Each day we make hundreds of tiny decisions that, when considered one at a time, appear harmless and insignificant. But when we begin to piece them together, take a step back and analyze them with an honest eye, a picture slowly begins to emerge.

• • • •

"It's not our abilities that show what
we truly are. It's our choices."

J.K. ROWLING
BRITISH AUTHOR OF THE HARRY POTTER SERIES

• • • •

The Child is unique, unlike any of the other 6 billion people on planet Earth. His life is a continuum of decisions, and his future is being created by the choices he makes today – and every day.

If he continues to strengthen and hone his talent, *plus* make optimum choices, he will become a talent-plus individual – one who stands out from the crowd. As he expresses his talents to fulfill human needs, he engenders the spark that fuels affluence.

Wisdom, the Child ponders, is the accurate consideration of the secondary sequence of events. For too long, however, he has only considered the first sequence of events that would result from his choices. Now he is more interested in the future and what steps he must take to effect positive and lasting change in the secondary sequence of events that results from the choices he makes.

Based on results thus far, the Child also realizes that while he has not often gotten what he wanted or needed, he has always gotten exactly what he unconsciously intended or expected. Had he truly intended to succeed thus far, and been willing to put in the time and effort to get there, he would be in a different place today.

••••

> "Your future is created by what
> you do today, not tomorrow."
>
> **ROBERT KIYOSAKI**
> AMERICAN AUTHOR AND ENTREPRENEUR

••••

He will mold new circumstances. His first decision is to quit smoking – a tough choice after many years of succumbing to nicotine addiction. He once longed for that quick fix (first sequence of events), but now the enlightened Child muses that his health and pocketbook would be much richer had he made a firm, uncompromising decision to quit years ago (second sequence of events). The moment he makes this decision, the Child senses a magical personal transformation.

This is the first of many calculated decisions to come in the face of many choices. Whatever the challenges or obstacles he will face, he silently vows to himself that he will overcome them. His personal mantra becomes, "*Do Whatever It Takes (DWIT)*." **The Child has become a Man.**

EDUCATION

The Man had been waiting for fate to chart his path. Yet at this very instant, he senses that the universe has, in some mysterious way, been inviting exploration: "*Carpe diem*. Seize the day." The time for taking control and taking action is now. Just like in chess, small moves pave the way for big ones. He doesn't know what he doesn't know, but he has an ardent urge to learn, grow and explore the unknown. He *will* figure it out.

••••

"You cannot teach a man anything;
you can only help him to find it within himself."

GALILEO
ITALIAN PHYSICIST AND ASTRONOMER

••••

He enrolls in college with some apprehension, but it is short-lived. His professors reintroduce him to concepts he once regarded as boring, futile and worthless. Now he sees these concepts in a new light. He begins to see how they apply to life – and to *his* life – and he nurtures those feelings of amazement and awe, feelings forgotten so long ago. He renews his commitment to himself and takes more classes, focusing on his studies with a zeal for learning and moving forward.

••••

"All learning has an emotional base."

PLATO
GREEK PHILOSOPHER AND MATHEMATICIAN

••••

In his psychology class, he sees *his* life pattern reflected in Abraham Maslow's human behavioral theory, which categorizes motivation into stages of needs. Maslow, he learns, studied exemplary people such as Albert Einstein, Jane Adams, Eleanor Roosevelt and Frederick Douglass, as well as the healthiest 1 percent of college students. To help others find meaning in their lives, Maslow summarized his

Transcendence
Self-actualization
Aesthetic Needs
Need to Know and Understand
Esteem Needs
Belongingness and Love Needs
Safety Needs
Physiological Needs

MASLOW'S Hierarchy of Needs

findings into the Hierarchy of Needs pyramid.

At the bottom are "deficiency needs," which, when absent, impair progression into a higher state of motivation until the need is satisfied. They include:

PHYSIOLOGICAL NEEDS

Oxygen,
Food,
Water,
Sex,
Sleep and
Excretion.

SAFETY NEEDS

With physical needs relatively satisfied, the individual's safety needs take precedence and dominate behavior. These include the security of:

Body,
Employment,
Resources,
Health and
Property.

SOCIAL NEEDS

After physiological and safety needs are fulfilled, belongingness and acceptance in social circles take the reins, including:

Friendship,
Intimacy and
Family.

ESTEEM NEEDS

The normal human desire to be accepted and valued by others, esteem needs exist on two levels, and deprivation of either can lead to an inferiority complex, weakness and helplessness.

Reputation (Lower Level):
Respect from others, status, recognition, fame, prestige and attention.

Self-Esteem (Higher Level):
Self-respect, strength, competence, mastery,
self-confidence, independence and freedom.

The Man begins to understand his motivational history and his present state of mind. He has progressed through the first four levels and now has the time and desire to progress to the next tier of motivation – "growth needs." The more the Man learns, the more he realizes that he does not know.

••••

"Personally, I'm always ready to learn, although I do not always like being taught."
WINSTON CHURCHILL
FORMER PRIME MINISTER OF GREAT BRITAIN

••••

NEED TO KNOW AND UNDERSTAND
With deficiency needs met, individuals begin to yearn for greater understanding, leading to a quest for more:

Knowledge,
Meaning and
Education.

The more the Man learns about the world, the more he appreciates all its splendors.

AESTHETIC NEEDS
Aesthetic needs are the desire to express oneself in ways that are creative, beautiful, artistic and/or pleasing. They include the appreciation of and search for:

Beauty,
Balance,
Form,
Order,
Symmetry,
Closure and
Structure.

He takes time to smell the roses and, in the process, realizes that he too is contributing to the artistry of life. He appreciates more fully the finer things, as well as Nature's simple beauties, and seeks to bring harmony and structure into his own life.

SELF-ACTUALIZATION AND TRANSCENDENCE

The ultimate goal of life, self-actualization is a higher psychic or spiritual state of development with visionary intuition, altruism and unity consciousness. Self-actualized people:

- Know exactly who they are, where they are going
  and what they want to accomplish;
- Realize and use their full potential, capacities and talents;
- Desire to become everything they are capable of becoming;
- Are free from caring what others think about them;
- Base decisions and actions not simply on the outcomes,
  but because it's their purpose in life;
- Are creative, spontaneous, original, inventive
  and less constricted than others;
- Accept their authentic selves;
- Are deeply democratic and lack prejudice;
- Have clear perceptions of facts and reality and are comfortable with it;
- Focus on problems outside themselves and are concerned
  with basic issues and eternal questions;
- Like privacy and enjoy periods of detachment from others for reflection;
- Rely on their own development and continued growth;
- Appreciate and are grateful for the basic pleasures of life;

· Experience a deep feeling of kinship with others; and
· Hold themselves to definite, high ethical and moral standards.

The Man asserts that he will strive to reach a self-actualization pinnacle. Curiously enough, the zenith of his pursuit requires (and magnifies) an intangible energy, one born of ideas and motivation, that is safely harbored between his ears; it is the power to move mountains. As his fate, purpose and destiny become clear, he realizes that he, and only he, has the ability to manifest that vision of the future – and it begins with a mindset change.

••••

"Imagination is everything.
It is the preview of life's coming attractions."
ALBERT EINSTEIN
THEORETICAL PHYSICIST AND PHILOSOPHER

••••

The Man begins to truly understand the meaning of:

Fully

Allowing

It

To

Happen

••••

"Faith is a sounder guide than reason.
Reason can only go so far, but faith has no limits."
BLAISE PASCAL
FRENCH MATHEMATICIAN AND PHYSICIST,
AND CATHOLIC PHILOSOPHER

••••

The Man has always lived in the here and now, relying on the principle that seeing is believing. So he has not believed in himself – in his capabilities and potential. But education has opened his eyes to whole new vistas and understandings of both the mind and the physical world. He has been looking at life but not getting the full picture; he has not been *seeing*.

Next, the Man takes Life Sciences and sees water – a ubiquitous commodity the Man has taken for granted – in a new light. Though he has known since childhood that people can't survive long without water, he learns now that no other nutrient deficiency has such profound effects on the human body. Without water, a person's blood pressure rises, the heart begins to malfunction and kidneys shut down.

He learns that water is *part* of him. His own lean muscle tissue contains about 75 percent water, his blood about 95 percent, his body fat about 14 percent and his bone about 22 percent.

He is reminded that water covers roughly 70 percent of the planet's surface, and while it is always in motion, there is no beginning or end to its cycle. At various times in this cycle, water changes states (from liquid to vapor to ice) many times, often in the blink of an eye. Although the balance of water on Earth remains fairly constant over time, individual water molecules come and go in a hurry.

Water, the Man muses, is unpretentious. It is not rocket science; it is a common, simple molecular structure of hydrogen and oxygen that has the power to give life, mold earth, wash our cars and bodies and provide play and relief from the heat. And it has the power to take life with its

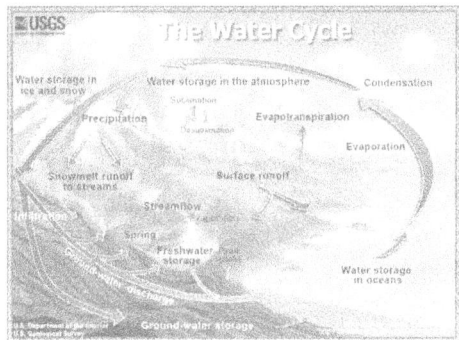

The Water Cycle

PRODUCED BY THE U.S. GEOLOGICAL SURVEY

hurricanes, tsunamis and floods. Frozen water in the form of glaciers and river torrents alike has carved mountains. The Grand Canyon, in all its splendor of rock and grandeur, was formed by the power of water in motion. It tumbles and polishes rocks, powers locomotives and generates enough electricity to power cities. Leveraged water carries gigantic payloads of cargo across great distances on every continent. The great Nile, the Mississippi, the Amazon, the Danube and the Yangtze remind the Man of historical moments of significance, as each of these majestic bodies has helped build civilizations, carried explorers to new lands, uncovered new species, driven climate changes and provided food, water and commerce for people.

"'I like geography best,' he said, 'because your mountains and rivers know the secret. Pay no attention to boundaries.'"

BRIAN ANDREAS
AMERICAN WRITER, PAINTER,
SCULPTOR AND PUBLISHER

••••

Yet the water in those majestic bodies is no different from the water that comes from his faucet. Water has direction; it has momentum. When heated, it expands and has the power to become invisible.

Water's intrinsic energy fascinates the Man. He is inspired – and on a mission to see clearly through the mental fog and into the unknown. He wants to uncover the hidden nuggets of the universe, just like a gold panner sifts the valuable mineral from the pay dirt. He wants to wash away the debris – the fluff within himself – and discover new realms, new potential.

On a camping outing with his Beloved and her family one clear spring day, the Man wakes up before everyone else and, upon hearing the rushing water of the nearby stream beckoning him, takes a solo walk down to its shores. In the distance, he can smell the inviting fire of fellow campers up the trail. On his trek he notices the woodpeckers busy at work, finding grubs and bugs in the trunks of trees with their rapid-fire rat-a-tat-tat. Butterflies and bees get an early start, methodically and gracefully lighting upon every blooming flower in sight. Colorful birds sing their wake-up songs, adding a unique harmony to the rushing water as it tumbles across the rocks, creating an alluring and entrancing melody.

He sits by the stream's edge, writing each of his woes into the sand with a broken twig, and watches as periodic waves wash away his fears of inadequacy. He feels an unexpected cleansing from this symbolic gesture.

He carefully cups a handful of water and notices how it quickly conforms to every contour, wrinkle and crevice in his hand. Yet while he has the intrinsic power to hold it, he also knows that should he jump in, the water's power would carry him off. The conundrum of this apparent disparity between a gentle, malleable liquid that he can hold and control in the palm of his hand in one moment, yet that could overpower his entire body in another, perplexes and fascinates him.

• • • •

> "The value of an education in a liberal arts college is not the learning of many facts, but the training of the mind to think something that cannot be learned from textbooks."
>
> **ALBERT EINSTEIN**
> THEORETICAL PHYSICIST AND PHILOSOPHER

• • • •

With his second family, the Man spends the rest of the day enjoying the water – swimming around in a safe cove downstream where the stream meets the river and then venturing forth in a canoe to a distant shore, gliding on the water's surface, powering himself with raw muscle as he directs the canoe and battles the river's drag.

The Man, his psyche renewed and full of awe, wants to become a steward of water. He will learn to apply its benefits wherever he goes.

Though he doesn't choose Life Sciences as his career, in its study he finds a talisman to catapult him into the realm of possibility. *Water and life are inseparable. Life cannot exist without water. Water cleanses and purifies. Yet water that stands still stagnates and putrefies. Water only gains its power by being in motion! The Man realizes that his life needs direction, momentum and "flavor."* Mediocrity has been flavorless and, at times, even bitter. The Man has found an analogy upon which he can build his life – unconventional thinking, to be sure, but it engenders new thought patterns, solutions and approaches. He has found a life metaphor!

• • • •

> "Water is the driving force of all nature."
>
> **LEONARDO DA VINCI**
> ITALIAN POLYMATH
> (PAINTER, SCULPTOR, ARCHITECT, MUSICIAN AND SCIENTIST)

• • • •

He will adopt the cleansing, polishing and transitive characteristics of a *Washer*, attributes akin to those of Niagara Falls or a wave traversing the seven seas – clear, sustainable energy in motion. He will:

- *Absorb* and seek out new fountains of knowledge;
- *Adapt* to new environments and make the best of each opportunity or circumstance presented;
- *Carry* responsibility, responsibly meeting every challenge in the best way he can;
- *Cleanse* his life and maintain himself in a dignified manner;
- *Create* new innovations and environments that help him and his communities;
- *Flow* with positive energy that continuously transforms himself and others;
- *Follow* through with his commitments;
- *Forge* new channels of discovery and possibility;
- *Give* sustenance to those in need;
- *Mold* and **shape** his destiny;
- *Nourish* the heartbeats of life;
- *Persist* in the face of roadblocks;
- *Polish* his skill with determination and practice;
- *Refresh* his psyche and **renew** his soul;
- *Tame* the torrents of life's challenges;
- *Wash* away obstacles that impair him from meeting objectives; and
- *Work* hard with plenty of sweat equity.

Simple, pragmatic guiding principles infuse new life, new energy. He discovers a newfound ability to lead change and be a force for progress as he ventures into the unknown.

····

"One must be something
in order to do something."
JOHANN WOLFGANG VON GOETHE
GERMAN WRITER AND POLYMATH

····

He knows it will not always be easy. Waves move forward, but they also experience the peaks and troughs that give the wave its actual form. He will always do his best, but his accomplishments may be different when he is on the crest of a wave versus when he is in the trough. He will accept this, so long as he continues to move forward, closer and closer to his goals.

His firm purpose emanates from the inside out. The Man stands for something; he has found a cause worth living for and, if necessary, dying for. He is cognizant that he can either get by, drive by or forge a new byway. He feels that, in a subtle way, he has the power to inspire, and to be inspired!

•••

wash (v):

To cleanse. To flow over, against or past. To carry, erode, remove or destroy by the action of moving water. To rid of corruption or guilt; cleanse or purify. To cause to undergo a swirling action. To hold up under examination; be convincing. To flow, sweep or beat with a characteristic lapping sound. To be carried away, removed or drawn by the action of water. To be revealed eventually. To turn out well in the end.

Source: *American Heritage Dictionary of the English Language, Fourth Edition, 2000*

SELF-AWARENESS

School, field trips, professional and social engagements and the like expand the Man's social circle. He now mingles with like-minded individuals who are visionary, disciplined and intrepid – who inspire and are inspired by him.

One night, as the Man travels across the desolate Death Valley National Park in California, he stops with his companions to take in the night sky and some fresh air. Without another soul in sight, it feels like they're in the middle of nowhere, like if not for the road they are on, they would be doomed with no escape.

The last person out of the van, the Man hears each person gasp as he or she exits the vehicle. As he steps out and his eyes adjust to the natural light, he understands their excitement. With no man-made light for miles, the night sky is illuminated with what looks like a million stars – more than any of them have ever seen at one time. He is bedazzled by the twinkling heavens and how they make the desert landscape visible even at night. He can pick out the North Star, and in the midst of all the glowing speckles, he can discern the Big Dipper's location, no longer camouflaged by the moon and urban skylines he has lived beneath.

As the Man marvels at the multitude of celestial bodies, a revelation settles in: These same stars helped guide Christopher Columbus, Marco Polo and other early explorers in their historical journeys. He feels connected to these risk-takers who forged into the unknown, suddenly understanding their scars and trials in a new way. He begins to recognize that, unbeknownst to him, the triumphs, pains and experiences of his own past – including his errant choices and the resistive forces within his mind – have been shaping him all along, instilling an inner fortitude that will sustain him, just as it did the early pioneers.

The Man feels kindred spirits. He feels empowered. His willpower (or *want*power) blossoms in the midst of fear and uncertainty. He will tap into this personal well of energy, venturing into his own uncharted territories. He, who had lost his direction, has now found his way.

Upon his return to civilization, the Man continues to read about great men and women in history. He collects their pearls of wisdom and creates a list of quotes about success – words that inspire him, words he can live by:

"Perpetual optimism is a force multiplier."
COLIN POWELL, FORMER U.S. SECRETARY OF STATE AND 4-STAR GENERAL

"Success is moving from one failure to another without losing enthusiasm!"
WINSTON CHURCHILL,
FORMER PRIME MINISTER OF GREAT BRITAIN, WRITER AND ARTIST

*"Ninety-nine percent of failures come from people
who have the habit of making excuses."*
GEORGE WASHINGTON CARVER,
AMERICAN SCIENTIST, BOTANIST AND EDUCATOR

*"The better a man is, the more mistakes he will make, for the more
new things he will try. I would never promote into a top-level job a man
who was not making mistakes ... Otherwise he is sure to be mediocre."*
PETER DRUCKER, AMERICAN WRITER AND MANAGEMENT CONSULTANT

*"I don't know the key to success,
but the key to failure is to try to please everyone."*
BILL COSBY, AMERICAN COMEDIAN, ACTOR AND AUTHOR

"It's not that I'm so smart, it's just that I stay with problems longer."
ALBERT EINSTEIN, GERMAN-BORN SWISS-AMERICAN
THEORETICAL PHYSICIST, PHILOSOPHER AND AUTHOR

*"I know fear is an obstacle for some people, but it is an illusion to me.
Failure always made me try harder next time."*
MICHAEL JORDAN, AMERICAN BASKETBALL PLAYER

*"One should not pursue goals that are easily achieved.
One must develop an instinct for what one can just barely
achieve through one's greatest efforts."*
ALBERT EINSTEIN

"Before success comes in any man's life, he is sure to meet with much temporary defeat and, perhaps, some failure. When defeat overtakes a man, the easiest and most logical thing to do is quit. That is exactly what the majority of men do."
NAPOLEON HILL, AMERICAN AUTHOR OF PERSONAL SUCCESS LITERATURE

"There are no secrets to success. It is the result of preparation, hard work and learning from failure."
COLIN POWELL

"To climb steep hills requires slow pace at first."
WILLIAM SHAKESPEARE, ENGLISH POET AND PLAYWRIGHT

"A woman is like a tea bag: You cannot tell how strong she is until you put her in hot water."
NANCY REAGAN, FIRST LADY OF THE U.S. FROM 1981 TO 1989

"If you risk nothing, then you risk everything."
GEENA DAVIS, ACTRESS, FILM PRODUCER, WRITER, MODEL AND FORMER OLYMPIC ARCHER

"Failure is simply the opportunity to begin again more intelligently."
HENRY FORD, AMERICAN INDUSTRIALIST WITH 161 PATENTS

"My hope still is to leave this world a bit better than when I got here."
JIM HENSON, CREATOR OF THE MUPPET SHOW AND SESAME STREET

"A pessimist sees the difficulty in every opportunity; an optimist sees the opportunity in every difficulty."
WINSTON CHURCHILL

"Let others lead small lives, but not you. Let others argue over small things, but not you. Let others cry over small hurts, but not you. Let others leave their future in someone else's hands, but not you."
JIM ROHN, PERSONAL DEVELOPMENT AUTHOR AND SPEAKER

"If you want the rainbow, you gotta put up with the rain."
DOLLY PARTON, SINGER-SONGWRITER, AUTHOR,
ACTRESS AND PHILANTHROPIST

"Talent develops in quiet places, character in the full current of life."
WOLFGANG AMADEUS MOZART,
GERMAN COMPOSER OF THE CLASSICAL ERA

*"The secrets of this earth are not for all men to see,
but only for those who will seek them."*
AYN RAND, RUSSIAN-AMERICAN NOVELIST AND PHILOSOPHER

*"Opportunity is missed by most because it is dressed
in overalls and looks like hard work."*
THOMAS EDISON, AMERICAN INVENTOR, SCIENTIST AND BUSINESSMAN

*"One can live magnificently in this world
if one knows how to work and how to love."*
LEO TOLSTOY, RUSSIAN NOVELIST

*"To do the useful thing, to say the courageous thing, to contemplate
the beautiful thing: That is enough for one man's life."*
T.S. ELIOT, ANGLO-AMERICAN POET AND PLAYWRIGHT

"If I had to live my life again, I'd make the same mistakes, only sooner."
TALLULAH BANKHEAD, AMERICAN ACTRESS,
TALK-SHOW HOST AND BON VIVANT

*"If you realized how powerful your thoughts are,
you would never think a negative thought."*
PEACE PILGRIM, AMERICAN PACIFIST AND PEACE ACTIVIST

*"People are like stained-glass windows. They sparkle and shine
when the sun is out, but when the darkness sets in, their true beauty
is revealed only if there is light from within."*
ELISABETH KÜBLER-ROSS,
SWISS SCIENTIST, DOCTOR, EDUCATOR AND MOTHER

"I cannot always control what goes on outside.
But I can always control what goes on inside."
DR. WAYNE DYER, SELF-DEVELOPMENT AUTHOR AND SPEAKER

"Those who are blessed with the most talent don't necessarily outperform
everyone else. It's the people with follow-through who excel."
MARY KAY ASH,
INSPIRATIONAL AUTHOR AND FOUNDER OF MARY KAY COSMETICS

"I am still determined to be cheerful and happy, in whatever situation
I may be; for I have also learned from experience that the greater part of our
happiness or misery depends upon our dispositions, and not our circumstances."
MARTHA WASHINGTON, THE FIRST FIRST LADY OF THE U.S.

Along with these great historical thinkers, all the business and self-help books the Man has read have revealed the importance of attitude, perseverance, leveraging knowledge and technology, education and utilizing the gifts with which genes and nature have blessed us. He posits on an end objective and what impact he wants to have – what difference he wants to make for himself and for his community.

To succeed he must help other people. He realizes that the greater his influence on the masses, directly or indirectly, the greater his success and resulting rewards. He muses over these elements and wonders how they can be combined into a mathematical algorithm to help predict his success and track his endeavors.

He discovers several formulas posited by business thinkers. Brian Tracy argues that human achievement is equal to innate attributes plus acquired attributes, times mental attitude. Denis Waitley and Tom Watson say success can be measured by doubling your failure rate. Paul Zane Pilzer, economic advisor to two former presidents, says that wealth equals your personal resources multiplied by your application of technology. And Earl Nightingale, who authored more than 7,000 radio and television commentaries and two best-selling books, asserts that only 5 percent of the population achieves an unusual level of success.

All these formulas have merit, decides the Man, but each seems incomplete alone. So he synthesizes the wisdom of many business leaders into the following algebraic equation:

$$\text{Success Potential} = \begin{array}{c} 5\% \text{ who} \\ \text{succeed} \\ \times \end{array} \left[\dfrac{\left[\text{Innate Attributes} + \text{Acquired Attributes}\right] \times \text{Technology} \times \text{Mental Attitude} \times \text{People You Know}}{\dfrac{\text{Number of Tries} - \text{Number of Failures}}{\text{Number of Tries}}} \right]$$

S_P = **Success Potential:** number of people who will reap *my benefits*

IA = **Innate Attributes:** advantages I was born with, such as health, speed, dexterity and memory

AA = **Acquired Attributes:** skills I have learned, been trained in and polished – such as my technical education, degree or specialized experience

T = **Technology:** my proficiency and application of such things as text messaging, standardized manufacturing procedures, international standards, e-mail, high-speed Internet, social networking, computers or new equipment, or software

NT = **Number of Tries Before Success**

NF = **Number of Failures Experienced** (always expressed as NT or NT-1)

MA = **Mental Attitude** (factors range from -1 to +1, as illustrated in the next chart)

P = **People:** those I know who can directly benefit from my product/service

The Man recognizes that each person possesses a personal well of energy – an internal fire that can heat, build and forge or burn, destroy and evaporate our dreams. This double-edged sword is attitude, and how we wield it is within our control. To evaluate his mental attitude, he uses this chart:

MA Factor	Mental Attitude
-1.0	Very negative
-0.8	Leave me alone

-0.6	Depressed
-0.4	Seems too hard
-0.2	Maybe I will get lucky
0.0	Neutral
0.2	Inclined to do something
0.4	Maybe others can help me
0.6	I can do it!
0.8	Willing to sacrifice time and money for my goal
1.0	Very positive

So what impact can the Man have in the world? To test his new theory – and calculate his own success potential – he creates nine scenarios and plugs the numbers into the formula:

EXAMPLES

ELEMENT	#1	#2	#3	#4	#5	#6	#7	#8	#9
IA	5	5	5	5	2	5	5	5	5
AA	2	2	2	2	5	2	2	2	2
T	2	2	2	2	2	2	2	2	2
NT	1	2	5	5	5	5	8	10	100
NF	0	1	4	4	4	5	7	9	99
MA	0	1	-0.4	0.2	1	1	1	1	1
P	1000	1000	1000	1000	1000	1000	1000	1000	1000
$SUCCESS_p$	0	1,400	-1,400	700	3,500	0	5,600	7,000	70,000

· Scenario #1: He is just starting out with a great idea, or so he thinks. This idea needs to be polished and critiqued. Though he knows 1,000 people his idea could benefit, he makes no impact.

· Scenario #2: He has learned from his first mistake and is excited. He has more confidence in his idea as he rolls it out a second time, and 1,400 could benefit if it is implemented.

· Scenario #3: He has honed his idea, but after four failures, his motivation and mental attitude are perceptibly negative. Word of his attitude spreads, and now even strangers are unwilling to listen to the potential merits of his idea. Now 1,400 people will shun him.

> YOUR TURN:
> *Use our calculator to evaluate your own Success Potential. Just visit wisherwasher.com and click the "Formula" tab.*

· Scenario #4: His skill and technology remain the same, but he adopts a more modest, positive outlook. People begin to take note, though some remain skeptical. He knows 1,000 people, but only 700 are likely to buy in.

· Scenario #5: He improves his attitude even more. His enthusiasm is contagious. His exuberance shines. If people understand the merits, they will spread the word for him, and he will impact far more people than he knows – up to 3,500 if his idea is implemented.

· Scenario #6: He remains positive in the midst of the realization that his idea needs more tweaks. He has encountered another temporary "failure."

· Scenario #7: He continues to persevere, and his heart remains optimistic, even after a few more tries and subsequent "failures." With each challenge, he gains more experience and insight. His potential impact continues to increase, setting him up for greater success when he finally strikes oil.

· Scenario #8: His input remains the same on every aspect, except his number of tries and failures. He's getting closer.

· Scenario #9: His determination, zeal and enthusiasm make him unstoppable. On his 100th try, he succeeds. How sweet it is to impact 70,000 people!

A keen awareness sets in that figments spawned in our imagination offer a preview of life's coming attractions. Our minds see what the eyes cannot, directing our moods and actions; using our heads is a great way to get ahead, as it is the most productive source for the wealth we yearn to build. His advantages – everything he needs to succeed – are safeguarded within the cauliflower-like structure of his brain, and he owns this asset free and clear!

••••

"The single most significant decision I can make on a day-to-day basis is my choice of attitude. It is more important than my past, my education, my bankroll, my successes or my failures, fame or pain, what other people think of me or say about me, my circumstances, or my position. Attitude is that 'single string' that keeps me going or cripples my progress. It alone fuels my fire or assaults my hope."

CHARLES R. SWINDOLL
SPIRITUAL LEADER, AUTHOR AND EDUCATOR

••••

He listens to the popular *Lead the Field* audio program in which Nightingale, who argued that only 5 percent of the population achieves real success, explains: "For the rest, average seems to be good enough. Most just seem to drift along, taking circumstances as they come, and perhaps hoping from time to time that things will get better." In other words, competitive pressures, weak willpower and life's natural screening process keep 95 percent of all people adrift in the Great Abyss of Average!

The Man, however, distinguishes himself from the crowd with his focused vision *and* originality. Unfettered by distractions, he relies on his DWIT attitude, which he reasons will separate him from the 95 percent who either fail to start, invest half-hearted attempts or give up.

He begins building his toolbox – organizing the gifts and advantages life bestowed upon him in his formative years, finally understanding that those circumstances will surely give him an edge in society. He takes a personal inventory of his natural talents (IA), acquired skills (AA) and the people he knows. He considers how he will leverage these strengths to ensure positive interactions with those he will meet, work with and help.

• • • •

"It took me a long time and much painful boomeranging of my expectations to achieve a realization everyone else appears to have been born with: that I am nothing but myself."

RALPH WALDO EMERSON
AMERICAN PHILOSOPHER AND POET

• • • •

Optimism had always seemed a bit naive to the Man, but now he understands that it can make or break him – that extraordinary people were once just ordinary people with extraordinary attitudes! He notices that his mental attitude (MA) is a multiplier in the success equation and that positive numbers in any other category can be negated by a pessimistic outlook. He will nurture and sustain a glass-half-full perspective.

Technology (T) is a multiplier as well, so if he can input a positive T, his success number is even greater, as is the number of people he can help. He vows to stay abreast of trends and technologies that can help him achieve his goals.

He is pleasantly surprised to find that age is not a factor in the formula, and he can find many examples to prove it. At age 13, Pablo Picasso was already a recognized artist. And Harland David ("Colonel") Sanders began Kentucky Fried Chicken franchise pursuit at age 65 using his first Social Security check.

Nor do background and environment preclude success. Horatio Alger's stories in the 1800s were based on real-life experiences of orphans. While many squander the riches they were handed at birth or fail to take advantage of the blessings life has bestowed on them, others who have not had the benefit of a safe home and loving family have succeeded tenfold. Honorable hard work, a clean, honest living and a little bit of luck can translate into a rags-to-riches story – and there are countless examples that exemplify this American dream.

••••

"I have not failed.
I've just found 10,000 ways that won't work."

THOMAS ALVA EDISON
PROLIFIC AMERICAN INVENTOR, SCIENTIST AND BUSINESSMAN
-RESPONSE TO THE SUGGESTION THAT HE FAILED AFTER 10,000
EXPERIMENTS TO DEVELOP A STORAGE BATTERY

••••

In his personal reading, listening and observing time, the Man learns to appreciate the fact that failure is inevitable – and that it happens even to the best of the best! Einstein's teachers told his parents he would never amount to anything. Thomas Edison went broke four times. Michael Jordan was cut from his high school basketball team. Steven Spielberg was put into a class for students with learning disabilities. *Chicken Soup for the Soul* creators Jack Canfield and Mark Victor Hansen were rejected by 144 publishers before getting their hugely successful series off the ground. Lucille Ball was dismissed from drama school with a note that read: "Wasting her time; she's too shy to put her best foot forward." Walt Disney was fired from a newspaper because he lacked imagination and had no original ideas. Michelangelo failed more than 200 times trying to produce the perfect sketch for the ceiling of the Sistine Chapel. Elvis Presley got a C in his high school music class. And in its first year, the Coca-Cola Company managed to sell only 400 bottles of Coke. The Man recognizes that if you've never failed, you've never lived. Life equals risk.

••••

"It doesn't matter if you try and try and
try again, then fail. It does matter if you try
and fail, and fail to try again."

CHARLES F. KETTERING
AMERICAN INVENTOR

••••

Amazingly, the more times we fail, the higher probability of success we have in the future, provided we persist. For every successful person he reads about, each "failure" allowed the individual to gain new insight and new experiences. Ironically, even failures can yield tangible and intangible winning nuggets –

like penicillin, cubic zirconium (synthetic diamonds) and the microwave, all accidental creations resulting from "failed" experiments.

• • • •

"It's only a failure if we fail to get the learning."
SCOTT COOK
FORMER INTUIT CHAIRMAN (#320 ON THE FORBES 400 IN 2005)

• • • •

The Man notices that his NT value will always be one number ahead of his NF if he is to attain his goal. He must try and fail – and then get up again. And he must repeat this cycle as many times as it takes.

He reads *The Medici Effect: What Elephants and Epidemics Can Teach Us About Innovation*, in which Frans Johansson notes that innovative people experience far more failures than their less creative counterparts because they pursue more ideas.

Johansson's lessons on how to succeed in the face of failure include:

- Failure to execute ideas is the GREATEST failure.
- Learn from past failures.
- Low failure rates mean you are not trying or are hiding information that can be of benefit.
- Look for people who have had intelligent failures and invite them to join your team!

• • • •

"The only people for me are the mad ones, the ones who are mad to live, mad to talk, mad to be saved, desirous of everything at the same time, the ones who never yawn or say a commonplace thing, but burn, burn, burn, like fabulous yellow roman candles exploding like spiders across the stars."
JACK KEROUAC
AMERICAN POET AND NOVELIST

• • • •

••••

"Life is an adventure; dare it."
MOTHER TERESA
NOBEL PEACE PRIZE WINNER

••••

The Man craves success, which to him means using his passion, talent and brainpower to create meaning in his life and to contribute to society. But what should his contribution be? What is his purpose on this planet?

He reads Nikos Mourkogiannis's *Purpose: The Starting Point of Great Companies.* Mourkogiannis explains how organizations – and individuals – that stand for something are the ones that create lasting competitive advantages. Successful companies can define their purpose in one of four key ways: Discovery of the new (IBM, Sony, 3M, Intel), Excellence (Berkshire Hathaway, Apple, BMW), Altruism (The Body Shop, Hewlett-Packard, Nordstrom) or Heroism (Ford, Microsoft, Exxon Mobil). With purpose as a foundation, planning, motivation and success flow freely.

So, he reasons, to define his strategy, he must choose his focus based on:

Pursuit of Discovery: *The lovers of the unknown*

Pursuit of Excellence: *The intrinsically beautiful and elegant*

Pursuit of Altruism: *The helpful; those with the urge to increase happiness in others*

Pursuit of Heroism: *The effective; those with the drive to achieve*

••••

"There are painters who transform the sun to a yellow spot, but there are others who with the help of their art and their intelligence transform a yellow spot into the sun."
PABLO PICASSO
SPANISH PAINTER AND SCULPTOR

••••

Purpose is a call to action that great leaders use to act consistently and decisively, innovating and building high-quality relationships, so his purpose must be aligned with his passion. The Man gravitates toward the purpose that sparks his inner core – his heart, desires and passions – noting that he will only pursue ethical, lawful and worthwhile goals. He will drive innovation that changes lives. The clarity this discovery brings is calming and energizing all at once.

The Man's confidence and certainty are now at an all-time high, and he feels invigorated in his quest. His creative spirit grows. Now is the perfect time to let his ideas flow and to put them into practice. He establishes a game plan, a road map of actions to take with timetables for accomplishment. He is judicious with his time and quickly becomes a force to be reckoned with.

••••

> "I would rather live life with those who attempt great things and fail than those who attempt nothing and succeed."
>
> **PAUL TSIKA**
> AMERICAN AUTHOR, SPEAKER AND PASTOR

••••

He learns in Malcom Gladwell's book *Outliers* that most success stories, from the Beatles to Bill Gates, invested more than 10,000 hours in their trade *before* they mastered those skills, and that their many hardships, setbacks and challenges gave them an edge: unparalleled experiences and practice of which the rest of the population can't boast. It allowed them to see firsthand the mistakes they made, the resolutions they implemented and the public's increased appreciation of their work. That practice is what made them great.

Bill Gates, founder of Microsoft, started programming in eighth grade, during the 1960s, when most *colleges* did not yet have computer labs. As a young lad, he worked at a lab where he and some cohorts ran up 1,575 hours of computer time in just seven months (that's about eight hours a day, seven days a week). In high school, he programmed on the weekends and snuck out in the middle of the night to work. No wonder he had the foresight to see the possibilities with software and computers! He hit 10,000 hours early.

The Beatles were turned down by a recording company, where one exec explained, "We don't like their sound, and guitar music is on the way out." Before their burst of success in 1964, the band performed an estimated 1,200 times in the not-so-posh districts – traveling from Liverpool, England, to Hamburg, Germany, five times between 1960 and 1962, performing 270 nights in just over a year and a half. In Hamburg, they often played for eight hours at a time. As John Lennon once put it, "We got better and more confident. We couldn't help it with all the experience playing all night long."

••••

"I hated every minute of training, but I said, 'Don't quit. Suffer now and live the rest of your life as a champion.'"
MUHAMMAD ALI
WORLD HEAVYWEIGHT BOXING CHAMPION

••••

Success does not come to those who just practice. It is *perfect* practice – with direction and a willingness to push the limits – that makes perfect. This is the edge that gives many their respective glory in the annals of history. Olympic athletes who win the medals usually finish ahead of their competitors by less than the blink of an eye (i.e., 0.02 seconds) – and that makes all the difference. Many are talented, but few have that winning edge that comes from perfect practice, perseverance, endurance and mental conditioning.

The Man hastens cultivation of *his* character strengths – virtues that extol positive personal values, animate his existence, guide his actions with integrity and stand the test of time. He makes a list of values with which to evaluate himself. Which does he possess, and which does he most need to cultivate?

Accepting	Active	Adaptable	Adventuresome	Aesthetic	Affectionate
Alive	Ambitious	Analytic	Appreciative	Articulate	Astute
Attentive	Attractive	Authoritative	Autonomous	Big-hearted	Bright
Businesslike	Calm	Careful	Caring	Centered	Challenge-oriented
Charming	Cheerful	Childlike	Clever	Colorful	Committed
Compassionate	Composed	Conceptual	Conscientious	Consistent	Constructive
Controlled	Convincing	Cool	Cooperative	Courageous	Creative
Curious	Daring	Decisive	Dedicated	Deep	Dependable
Detailed	Determined	Devoted	Dignified	Diligent	Diplomatic
Direct	Dominant	Dramatic	Driving	Durable	Dynamic
Earthy	Effective	Efficient	Empathetic	Enchanting	Energetic
Enlightening	Entertaining	Enthusiastic	Ethical	Evolving	Exciting
Expressive	Facile	Fair	Faithful	Fanciful	Fearless
Fiery	Flamboyant	Flexible	Fluent	Forceful	Forthright
Fun-loving	Generous	Giving	Goal-oriented	Good-natured	Graceful

Grounded	Gutsy	Hard-working	Helpful	Heroic	Honest
Honorable	Humorous	Idealistic	Imaginative	Incisive	Independent
Indomitable	Influential	Innovative	Insightful	Inspirational	Intellectual
Intense	Interesting	Intimate	Intuitive	Inventive	Investigative
Involved	Just	Knowledgeable	Lively	Logical	Loving
Loyal	Lucid	Magnetic	Memorable	Money-wise	Moral
Motivated	Natural	Noble	Nurturing	Observant	Open
Optimistic	Orderly	Organized	Outgoing	Outspoken	Patient
Perfectionist	Persevering	Persuasive	Philosophical	Physical	Pioneering
Playful	Poised	Polished	Positive	Powerful	Pragmatic
Precise	Productive	Professional	Progressive	Protective	Prudent
Quick	Realistic	Reasonable	Receptive	Resilient	Resolute
Resourceful	Responsible	Romantic	Rousing	Sagacious	Seasoned
Secure	Self-aware	Self-confident	Self-expressive	Self-reliant	Self-sufficient
Sensitive	Sensuous	Service-oriented	Shrewd	Sincere	Skillful
Socially Adept	Socially Responsible	Solid	Sophisticated	Soulful	Spirited
Spiritual	Spontaneous	Stable	Steadfast	Stimulating	Strong-willed
Structured	Successful	Sunny	Supportive	Tasteful	Technical
Tenacious	Thorough	Tireless	Tough	Trustworthy	Unassuming
Undaunted	Unpretentious	Unselfish	Up-to-date	Versatile	Vibrant
Vigorous	Visionary	Vivacious	Warm-hearted	Well-grounded	Well-liked
Witty	Worldly	Youthful			

The values he identifies will serve as a compass, helping him to navigate life's opportunities.

His propensity for the pursuit of understanding – and excellence – is magnetic. He will build a future instead of polishing his past. In parallel, he commits to try and right some of the wrongs of the past by apologizing to those he has hurt or disappointed, repaying debts and sending "Thinking of You" cards with a few heartfelt words.

Ideas may be intangible forces, as elusive as water vapor on a windy day. But with cool, solid determination, he feels empowered to transform the untouchable, the unseen, into a physical manifestation that reveals his gifts to the world. Whether it's a new product or service, or a kind word and a smile, he is a creator, transforming mental imagery into reality.

Recognizing that life is finite, he wonders what his epitaph will be. To make the impact he wants to make, he decides he must first plan what that would look like, so he writes out exactly what his tombstone will read if he accomplishes his mission in life:

My dry bones may lay here silently at rest, but my thoughts,
insights and dreams live on in the minds of many.
Generations will come and go, and yet my energy will charge on.
*I loved, failed and succeeded in uncharted waters. **I am a Washer!***

••••

"Time is limited, so I better wake up
every morning fresh and know that I have
just one chance to live this particular
day right, and to string my days together
into a life of action and purpose."

LANCE ARMSTRONG
DISGRACED TOUR DE FRANCE WINNER

••••

Our Man no longer wants to sit on the sidelines, or in his La-Z-Boy, watching others fulfill their dreams. He is no longer content to experience their dreams vicariously by watching others and reading self-help books. They have been good teachers, and while he knows he will always be learning from others, he's also ready to graduate, to become a *doer*, to make something happen for *him*. Picasso's estimated 50,000 artworks, Mozart's 600 musical composition works, Mother Teresa's $1 billion organization operating 600 facilities in 130 countries, and Helen Keller's 19 books are proof that some blaze trails, while the vast majority are mere spectators and consumers of life. Getting by, making enough just to consume, is adding riches and meaning to others' lives and not his own.

Before, our Man came up with 5,000 excuses and not one valid reason to chart his own course. He smugly criticized the success of others and rarely took heed of their counsel, because he was on the fast track to ... apparently nowhere. He realizes now that the condescending opinions he shared so confidently and freely were vain attempts to hide his own insecurities and lack of achievement. No more!

He will seek and accept advice from those he admires so that he can avoid reinventing the wheel, while keeping his eyes open to opportunities beyond the evident. Those who can see through the visible, he affirms, can achieve the impossible. He will do the impossible!

He needs an environment and a change in perspective. He reflects on fishing as a young lad and how his Father taught him that to get the big fish, he needed to find the right spot (one in the deep, clean waters where the big fish thrive), have the right gear and offer the right incentive. When he cast his rod along the sandy shores of a murky pond, he only caught nibbling minnows that could hardly satiate his appetite. Likewise, even though today his appetite for success is voracious, he continues to mingle with the minnows – both by surrounding himself with some individuals who do not promote his own personal growth and by doubting himself. Small minds yield small results, so he must think and act big – with the proper attitude, attire, perseverance and education – so that he too can reel in "the big one."

••••

"At least this will be my chance to find out if I am who I think I am, or if I just hope; if I am going to do what I have taught myself is right, or if I am just going to wish I were."

WILLIAM FAULKNER
NOBEL PRIZE-WINNING AMERICAN AUTHOR

••••

With his growing body of knowledge, coupled with his own applied creative ingenuity, our Man achieves a genuine specialization in the universe. He offers substance and value in his chosen field. He has discovered the fun in finding the nuggets hidden within his being and within his work. His social network continues to expand, and consequently his circle of influence enlarges. The world judges his contributions with admiration and pleasure.

He now attracts men and women from all walks of life who *want* to work with him. His foresight and clarity of thought are practical as well as innovative. He is becoming a leader. As he enriches the lives of others, he makes a genuine difference. In return, his own riches multiply. Paradoxically, the more he gives, the more he receives.

••••

"Rome was not built in a day."
LATIN PROVERB

••••

Through his determination, he has become a fortune-teller of his own existence. He dictates his future and creates his fortunes.

Quietly and consistently, the sun and the moon continue to revolve, traversing an ever-expanding universe. The routines of the universe, however, do not seem so routine anymore. Our Man sees that he too can expand his horizons if he is consistent – and persistent. Gone are the days when he lamented, "I have no time." He has learned the basics of prioritizing his work by eliminating the many nonproductive time stealers that do not further his mission. An informed and evolved Man, he accomplishes much, much more (in much less time) by focusing on the things he truly wants to do. Time passes quickly, but it has been time well spent, as he now has much to show for his labor.

DECISION POINT

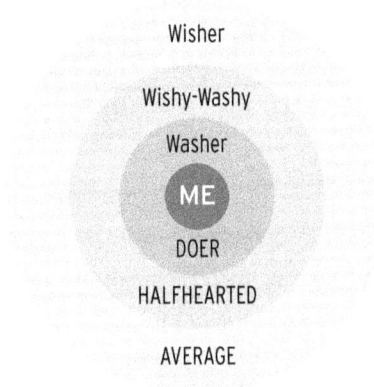

Wisher

Wishy-Washy

Washer

ME

DOER

HALFHEARTED

AVERAGE

What will my aim be?

*How many earned arrows must be stocked
in our quiver to hone in on the reward?*

• • • •

"The greater danger for most of us lies not in setting our aim too high and falling short, but in setting our aim too low and achieving our mark."

MICHELANGELO
ITALIAN ARTIST AND SCULPTOR

• • • •

FAMILY

Though he has been blessed with the wisdom of many mentors who have helped groom our Man for professional success, he realizes that there is one resource he has not utilized. He is enthusiastic about his external quest but senses the need for an internal edge. Our Man succumbs to an inner craving that has been repressed for too long by work and too many social engagements: the need to converse with his Father about life, about *his* purpose in life.

He soon gets the perfect opportunity, as one evening he finds his Father reading in his usual leather, high-back chair. Our Man smiles and shakes his head as he recalls the many times he's encouraged his Father to replace this chair with the latest model – the one with heated seats, massagers, electric cup holders and a built-in remote control – but his Father always refused to replace this relic. Today, as our Man sees the chair, which like his Father reflects years of wear from a long lifetime of providing comfort, support and service for others, he gets it and vows to make sure it never gets thrown away.

• • • •

"A father is someone you look up to no matter how tall you grow."
AUTHOR UNKNOWN

• • • •

Sitting by the crackling fireplace, a cup of warm coffee at his side, the Father seems relaxed and meditative – an opportune time for this conversation. Our Man asks, "Dad, can I talk to you?"

His Father peers over his reading glasses, lays down his book and responds, "Sure, son, what about?"

Our Man opens his mouth but finds that he doesn't even know where to start. Seeing his son struggle for the words to begin what he hopes will lead to a heart-to-heart chat between father and son – adult to adult – the Father begins: "Son, do you know what I want you to be?"

"A success in my own field?"

"Yes, and I'm very proud of your accomplishments," he responds. *"But most of all, I want you to be better than I was."*

It seems like such a simple statement, yet it is so profound that our Man's eyes well up with tears of joy and pride. There is no competition or remorse in his Father's voice, only a loving wish for a better tomorrow for our Man, his future family and generations to come. Our Man has never before seen clearly the value of his Father's patience, understanding and "Rock of Gibraltar" protection of the family. He has been leading by example all along. The ability to not just live, but to make a life and improve the lives of the generations he spawns, is mankind's greatest gift. Life has forward momentum.

The Father tells his son about Napoleon Hill, a once-impoverished reporter who interviewed 500 of America's richest people at the turn of the century. In his research, he identified 13 attributes that these successful people embodied, which he recorded in his book, *Think and Grow Rich*. This book made Hill a millionaire and served the Father well in recent years. Our Man listens as his Father reads the 13 principles:

· Desire: **The starting point of all achievement.**
· Faith: **Visualization of and belief in the attainment of desire.**
· Autosuggestion: **The medium for influencing the subconscious mind.**
· Specialized Knowledge: **Personal experiences or observations.**
· Imagination: **The workshop of the mind.**
· Organized Planning: **The crystallization of desire into action.**
· Decision: **The mastery of procrastination.**
· Persistence: **The sustained effort necessary to induce faith.**
· Power of the Master Mind: **The driving force of many.**
· Sexual Transmutation: **A healthy libido.**
· The Subconscious Mind: **The connecting link to our inner selves.**
· The Brain: **The broadcasting and receiving station for thought.**
· The Sixth Sense: **The door to the temple of wisdom.**

A quote from Hill – "Whatever the mind of man can *conceive*, and *believe*, he can *achieve*" – resonates and strikes a chord within our Man. He vows to read this book. Even Mother Nature seems to silently harbor this basic secret. After all, nothing about a caterpillar even hints that it will become a butterfly – but it does.

For so long, our Man has been hastily searching for answers, but as he observes his Father, he sees that untold riches were right in front of him all along. The years of laughter, trips, counsel, support and guidance have slipped by – largely unnoticed, taken for granted and unappreciated. Our Man chalked up all those selfless acts of caring, discipline, hardship and tutelage as merely a father's duty, but he is now overcome with gratitude and admiration.

What's more, he could have learned so much about business from his Father, had he ever bothered to ask. Now that he takes the time to consider his Father's profession, he remembers the periods of boom and periods of bust his business went through – and how he quickly adapted each time to the new circumstances, keeping his business *and* family strong through it all.

••••

> "Feeling gratitude and not expressing it is like wrapping a present and not giving it."
> **WILLIAM ARTHUR WARD**
> AMERICAN WRITER

••••

Suddenly he doesn't know how he could possibly express his admiration and gratitude, but he tries anyway, telling his Father how much his sacrifices, wisdom and love mean to him – and how sorry he is that he ever took those things for granted. Neither man can contain his tears of joy for the opportunity to finally see clearly into one another's souls – and for the pride at what they've each found.

The Mother enters the room just in time to witness their embrace and cries with joy, for the two loves of her life have effortlessly broken down barriers and façades built up over many years. She knew this day would come, when her son would once again look at his Father with the admiration he deserves. And her unwavering faith has finally paid off.

Our Man welcomes his Mother into their embrace, glad to see her, because he has a confession to make. He has watched these two loving people work, cry and laugh together his entire life. Their commitment and resolve have inspired him and set an example he is proud to follow. "I'm going to propose."

Though they knew it was coming (each progressive family dinner, picnic outing or trip to the mall made it clear that his Beloved would soon be their new "daughter"), they *both* succumb to tears of pride and joy. "So, tell me your secret," he says. "How have you stayed happy together for so long?"

Forseeing a dependable, responsible and trustworthy husband and father standing before them, they want their son to have an edge, to know that in marriage, words and ceremonies alone will not bridge the union. Intimacy (or "into-me-u-c") describes the depth of shared future vision, partnership, closeness, passion, communication and *friendship* that successful couples must build. This intimacy must be forged with trust, understanding and appreciation, the Father explains. And it must be regularly communicated.

••••

"Lust is easy. Love is hard.
Like is most important."
CARL REINER
AMERICAN FILM ACTOR, WRITER, DIRECTOR AND PRODUCER

••••

The Father scours the shelves of his library for a special book – *Five Love Languages: How to Express Heartfelt Commitment to Your Mate* by Gary Chapman. When he finally spots it and pulls it off the shelf, he notes its tattered edges – proof that it has been a good reference over the years. As he passes the torch to his son, he explains that the book will offer insight into the distinct dialects understood by the heart and processed by the mind to bond two individuals. He encourages his son to learn to practice them all, but that he and his soon-to-be fiancée should spend time identifying each other's preferred Love Languages and then practice them regularly.

1. **Words of Affirmation:** Verbal appreciation speaks powerfully to those with this primary Love Language. Simple expressions of gratitude (e.g., "thank you for cleaning up today") or compliments (e.g., "that suit looks great on you") are often all these people need to feel loved. Words of encouragement help them overcome insecurities and develop greater confidence in themselves and their relationships.

2. **Quality Time:** This requires more than mere proximity. It's about focusing all your energy on your mate. Watching sports while talking to one's spouse does not count as quality time – especially for those who prefer this Love Language. Quality conversation and the ability to be a sympathetic listener are very important in a healthy relationship. And just spending time together, doing things both people enjoy – whether

that's sitting on the couch or playing tennis in a couples league – brings a couple closer and, in the years to come, fills a shared memory bank both will treasure.

••••

"The problem with communication is the illusion that it has occurred."

GEORGE BERNARD SHAW

IRISH SOCIALLY CONSCIOUS PLAYWRIGHT

••••

3. **Receiving Gifts:** Those who speak this Love Language require gifts (even small ones), which they treasure as expressions of love and devotion. The gift of self – whether that's one's physical body or simply being there for that person, experiencing the same trials and success – is also an important symbol of love.

4. **Acts of Service:** Sometimes simply doing chores around the house can be viewed as an undeniable expression of love. It requires some degree of planning, time, effort and energy – all to make one's partner happy. And forget the stereotypes. Acts of service require *both* mates to humble themselves into performing some chores and services that aren't usually expected from their genders.

••••

"You can't make footprints in the sands of time sitting down."

AUTHOR UNKNOWN

••••

5. **Physical Touch:** Many individuals feel most loved when they receive physical contact. For a mate who speaks this Love Language loudly, it can make or break the relationship. Sexual intercourse is a big part of that, but it is only one dialect of physical touch. Many parts of the body are extremely sensitive to stimulation, and it is important to discover how one's partner responds to each, both physically and psychologically. Often a hug, kiss or held hand is enough. All marriages will experience crises. In these cases, a hug can communicate an immense amount of love. A person who prioritizes physical touch would much rather be held in silence than offered advice.

After explaining these principles and handing his son the book, the Father sums it up: "If you understand one another's differences, appreciate each other's roots, and are willing to make the petty sacrifices necessary to show love in the way each of you wants to be shown, such as opening the door for her or going grocery shopping with a smile, I have no doubt that your relationship will be a healthy one."

••••

"Married couples who love each other tell
each other a thousand things without talking."
CHINESE PROVERB

••••

A poem by John Piper, slipped within the worn pages of the book, gives further insight:

Love is the compassion that cares, the care that gets involved,
the commitment that sticks with a people through thick and thin!
Love is risk-taking when the flesh says look out for number one first.
Love is silence – when the words would hurt.
It is patience – when your neighbor's curt.
It is deafness – when scandal flows.
It is thoughtfulness – for others' woes.
It is promptness – when stern duty calls.
It is courage – when misfortune falls.
Love ever gives, forgives and outlives,
Ever stands with open hands.
And while it lives, it gives, for this is love's prerogative –
To give, and give, and give!

The Father congratulates him once again, and our Man finally manages to escape his Mother's emotional embrace. As he walks to his car, the Parents watch him out the window, arms encircled around one another's waists, both remembering the day he was born, filled with pride at the man he has become.

LEADERSHIP

Books have piqued our Man's interest for some time now, as they have provided a forum in which he can carry on silent conversations at will with great thinkers and leaders of the past and learn their stories, challenges and triumphs. This knowledge gives our Man a foundation, a place upon which he can begin to build his CASTLE, a principle stemming from the book *Inspire: What Great Leaders Do* by Lance Secretan. It encourages:

C*ourage*   He pledges to be more courageous.

A*uthenticity* He commits to showing up and being present in all aspects of life, removing the mask and becoming a real, vulnerable and intimate human being.

S*ervice*   He will serve others and the planet first - and himself second.

T*ruth-telling* He will be passionate about and committed to the truth and refuse to compromise his integrity or deny what he believes.

L*ove*   He will love more every day; it is his way to inspire others.

E*ffectiveness* He will become more effective in all aspects of life.

This CASTLE is a mantle, a solid platform for personal growth and a means to develop, enhance and expand his leadership skills. Our Man has gone through many calendars in his life – creating moments that he will treasure forever and others he wouldn't mind forgetting. Surprisingly, though, all of these experiences – good and bad – have illustrated new meaning, given him new exposures, honed his skills and expanded his horizons. He has developed his own branch of thought and welcomes the opportunity to share it with those willing to listen.

Others see this in him and respond by asking for his advice and mentorship, respecting his guidance and following his lead. He cultivates even more formidable relationships where synergistic seeds can germinate in the not-so-distant future. This activity requires time, caring and involvement. After all, he has learned that no one cares how much you know until they know how much you care. He memorizes people's birth names and becomes adept at pronouncing them in their native tongues, for he knows that human beings' most valuable possessions are the names bestowed upon them by their parents. Our Man appreciates this extraneous bond, this connection, this ancestry.

Inspiration comes from the most unlikely places. He learns that Oprah Winfrey, at just seven years of age, often recited the poem *Invictus* by William Ernest Henley. It resonates with him as well, the last two lines in particular:

> *Out of the night that covers me,*
> *Black as the pit from pole to pole,*
> *I thank whatever gods may be*
> *For my unconquerable soul.*
>
> *In the fell clutch of circumstance*
> *I have not winced nor cried aloud.*
> *Under the bludgeonings of chance*
> *My head is bloody, but unbowed.*
>
> *Beyond this place of wrath and tears*
> *Looms but the Horror of the shade,*
> *And yet the menace of the years*
> *Finds and shall find me unafraid.*
>
> *It matters not how strait the gate,*
> *How charged with punishments the scroll,*
> ***I am the master of my fate:***
> ***I am the captain of my soul.***

Nelson Mandela lived these words, exemplifying their possibilities. After 27 years in prison, he became president of South Africa at age 76, continuing the quest he embarked upon four decades earlier and succeeding by forging a democratic, nonracial South Africa that abolished apartheid. In November

2009, the United Nations General Assembly announced that Mandela's birthday, July 18, will now be known as Mandela Day to mark his contribution to world freedom.

••••

"We are blind until we see that in the human plan nothing is worth the making if it does not make the man. Why build these cities glorious if man unbuilded goes — in vain we build the world unless we know the builder grows."

EDWIN MARKHAM
AMERICAN POET

••••

Our Man sees scores of individuals who continue to build enjoyment, innovation and service to the masses. Do these people lead others by command, or do they lead by followership? Those who have led by command (e.g., Hitler, Stalin, Hussein) invariably fall, and those who lead by selfless inspiration and motivation become our heroes (e.g., Mandela, Gandhi, Kennedy). They become rich and successful, and yet, even when they could afford to just enjoy an idle, "easy" life, they continue to work in their passions.

They have earned the merit badge of leadership. They draw energy, willpower, insight and commitment from the exceptional people with whom they surround themselves and leverage those teams to achieve uncommon feats. They are bolstered by strong belief systems, solid values, superb ethics, original character, enviable knowledge, tested skills and, above all, an appreciation for people and the respect, compassion, drive and persistence each of us deserves.

••••

"You do not lead by hitting people over the head – that's assault, not leadership."

DWIGHT D. EISENHOWER
34TH PRESIDENT OF THE U.S.

••••

Leaders, he knows, embody a magnetic energy and openness that attracts individuals from very diverse backgrounds, skill bases, belief systems and cultures. Over time, they quietly and methodically build reservoirs of trust, insight and care in the people they meet, manage or support – one person at a time. He understands that we are all citizens of the world, connected by our commonalities and made stronger by our differences.

Our Man realizes that the word "leadership" is an acronym for the basic attributes that attract admiration and loyalty from the teams – all of which emphasize giving over getting. He understands that *giving* encourages others to give of themselves in return, allowing him to channel the pride, energy, sweat and sacrifice of many to achieve a *tour de force*.

••••

"The greatest good you can do for another is not just to share your riches but to reveal to him his own."

BENJAMIN DISRAELI
BRITISH STATESMAN

••••

Our Man exudes these essential and distinctive elements:

L *earning* — Reading, experiencing, asking questions, talking less and listening more; having a global mindset.

E *nthusiasm* — Knowing that positive attitudes are contagious; cherishing and rewarding your team; having fun along the way.

A *uthenticity* — Saying what you do and doing what you say; being open, approachable and understanding of mistakes.

D *irection* — Understanding your mission, setting the course for the future and communicating your vision.

E *xecution* — Being the executive on the plan; driving for effective performance and getting the job done.

R *espect* — Valuing diversity and innovation; building caring and empathetic relationships; appreciating work/life balance.

S*tructured*	Recognizing and building your own knowledge base and that of your team; giving people the tools, training and resources they need to do their jobs; being disciplined, yet flexible to listen and respond.
H*umility*	Recognizing that everyone contributes; not being showy or obtrusive; speaking more of the "we" than the "I" in the equation.
I*ntegrity*	Being sincere, fair, equitable and honest; practicing moral soundness.
P*assion*	Creating work environments that inspire excellence and build trust and pride.

••••

"The first method for estimating
the intelligence of a ruler is to look
at the men he has around him."
NICCOLO MACHIAVELLI
ITALIAN PHILOSOPHER AND POLITICIAN

••••

Our Man focuses his leadership efforts on *individuals*. He does not prejudge people based on their outer packaging – their backgrounds, appearances or differences from him. He knows that in order to have the highest-performing team working toward his vision, he must have a diverse team that knows how to leverage each other's strengths.

••••

"There is no limit to what a man can do or where he
can go if he doesn't mind who gets the credit."
RONALD REAGAN
40TH PRESIDENT OF THE U.S.

••••

He recalls hearing a story about Andrew Carnegie, the richest man in America at the turn of the last century. A reporter had asked him how he became such a success, and Carnegie replied that he made it by employing the best people in the business, people who were much better than him. The perplexed reporter then asked, "If you have better people than you working for you, then what is your role?"

Carnegie replied, *"My sole charge is to maintain the harmony among the minds."* This is the type of leader our Man wants to be! He must create an environment where ideas can be cross-fertilized. It must, he decides, be one of:

T*ogetherness* Working together rather than as an individual, knowing you can make things happen more easily and professionally.

E*mpathy* Relating to fellow employees; feeling concern about their well-being and an understanding of who they are - both on a personal and a professional level.

A*ssistance* Desiring and being able to help others who need a hand.

M*aturity* Being mature and fair in handling problems and challenges in a positive, constructive manner.

W*ork* Getting the job done - meeting deadlines, delivering the service and winning the game.

O*rganization* Being professionally organized to reduce crisis situations with the help of other employees and departments.

R*espect* Appreciating the strengths and diversity of the people you work with on a daily basis.

K*indness* Having compassion for and empowering all the people with whom you come into contact.

In Warren Bennis's book *On Becoming a Leader,* our Man learns the difference between a manager and a leader:

· The manager administers; the leader *innovates*.
· The manager is a copy; the leader is an *original*.
· The manager maintains; the leader *develops*.

- · The manager focuses on systems and structure;
  the leader *focuses on people*.
- · The manager relies on control; the leader *inspires trust*.
- · The manager accepts reality; the leader *investigates* it.
- · The manager has a short-range view;
  the leader has a *long-range perspective*.
- · The manager asks how and when; the leader asks *what and why*.
- · The manager has his or her eye always on the bottom line;
  the leader has his or her *eye on the horizon*.
- · The manager imitates; the leader *originates*.
- · The manager accepts the status quo; the leader *challenges* it.
- · The manager is the classic good soldier;
  the leader is *his or her own person*.
- · The manager does things right; the leader does the *right thing*.

••••

"You spend the first 40 years of your life
trying to be successful and the next 40 years
of your life trying to be significant."

BOB BUFORD
AMERICAN BUSINESS LEADER AND SOCIAL ENTREPRENEUR;
COFOUNDER OF THE LEADERSHIP NETWORK

••••

Success is a personal and social achievement that involves many people. The act of communicating energetically, succinctly and professionally is an art that our Man realizes he must master to become more effective. People yearn to hear his ideas and learn from his persona; they seek his attention and respect. The ability to articulate ideas, inspire, build relationships and live a life of integrity is a magnetic leadership trait that spawns more opportunities. Our Man exemplifies these virtues, energizing those around him.

••••

"No man is good enough to govern
another man without that other's consent."

ABRAHAM LINCOLN
16TH PRESIDENT OF THE U.S.

••••

To interact with others, he must be able to communicate effectively. The substance and delivery of his messages must be in sync so the public can see, feel and believe the essence of the truth he has to share. Many want to be led, but our Man is cognizant that he must first earn the right to lead.

He knows there are roughly 600,000 words in the English language, and yet the vast majority of people use only 2,000 in daily speech. Many studies have proven that people with superior vocabularies earn more and are more successful professionally because they can communicate more concepts, thoughts and feelings.

Earl Nightingale illustrated this well-established fact by analyzing the results of a vocabulary test administered to college graduates. He then followed their careers and earning levels over the next 20 years to see if there was any correlation between their word power and earning power. The result? As he puts it: "Without a single exception, in every case, those who had scored highest on the vocabulary test given in college were in the top income group, while those who had scored the lowest were in the bottom income group."

But our Man knows he'll need more than an outstanding vocabulary to succeed in his endeavor. People have different backgrounds, cultures, experiences, understandings and expectations. To reach the masses, he will need to tailor his message to each respective audience – on an individual level or on a large scale – recognizing that faith, tradition and customs demand it.

••••

"My goal for myself is to reach the highest level of humanity that is possible to me."

OPRAH WINFREY
TELEVISION HOST, PRODUCER AND PHILANTHROPIST

••••

He will need to find common ground between himself and his audience – and yet address them in the way that will make the greatest impact. Some audiences will want to know the bottom-line facts as quickly as possible, where others may want to know about and like *him* before they are willing to accept his ideas. Some will focus on the product, while others will consider first his character, compassion and integrity. One size does not fit all. This is the beauty of life: that it takes all kinds to make the world go round.

• • • •

"Discover that the most powerful way to help those you love is to lead by example – and realize you're leading by example all of the time."

JOE CARUSO
AUTHORITY ON HUMAN DEVELOPMENT AND TRANSFORMATION

• • • •

Our Man has a burning desire for *his* difference to make a difference! He wants to break new ground, tread down the unbeaten paths, climb the obstinate mountains and forge new schools of thought. He needs a team to accomplish what he alone cannot. His conviction and enthusiasm will "speak" through his body language, reinforcing his spoken words. He knows he must be realistic and persistent in his own timelines and expectations so that people see the potential of his vision and can adopt it – *want* to adopt it!

Sometimes compromise will be his best ally, representing the difference between a solution that gets implemented and one that could have been; win-win is possible, and it is his ultimate pursuit!

• • • •

"Every man is enthusiastic at times. One man has enthusiasm for thirty minutes, another man has it for thirty days. But it is the man who has it for thirty years who makes a success of his life."

EDWARD B. BUTLER
AMERICAN BUSINESSMAN

• • • •

SUCCESS

Over the course of time, our Man has experienced many trials, errors and set-backs, discovering in the process an inner purpose and a keen revelation of his personal cause. The inherent energy in his momentum has drawn in new (previously obscured) experiences, people, options and vantage points. The crises that the winds of change have ushered in and out have been cleverly disguised opportunities. His sails, however, were set to leverage the wind in his favor.

••••

"Give a man a fish, feed him for a day;
teach a man to fish and you feed him for a lifetime."
CHINESE PROVERB

••••

His journey has offered many easy outs, where others would have found excuses to take the first off-ramp. He heard what others said to him but remained in tune with his own inner voice. He chose to take the off-beaten path – one wrought with unknown twists and turns. A journey of a thousand miles always begins with the first step, and that was the hardest one to take. But he braved the unknown, the self-doubt and the odds, taking one courageous step after another, slowly increasing his speed, determination and focus. He has remained in control, meeting all the circumstances with which life presented him with resolve and fixed intention.

••••

"We must be the change
we wish to see in the world."
MAHATMA GANDHI
POLITICAL AND SPIRITUAL LEADER OF INDIA

••••

Our Man's transformation has marked the dawn of a sage age in the Information Age; he has become wiser at the same time that technology has made available a plethora of information his ancestors could only have dreamed of – and that's a powerful combination. His actions are methodical and effective, his contributions have meaning, and his unique achievements are stellar. He makes exemplary contributions to his profession, the public welfare and humanity, all the while maintaining a magnetic sense of humility. The sacrifices he has chosen to make have yielded magnificent rewards – for himself and others.

Despite his success, our Man does not become stagnant or complacent – content to step back and enjoy the fruits of his labor, letting someone else do all the heavy lifting. Instead, his burning desire for a *cause* and his belief that he can make a difference – that he owes it to himself and the world – only grow stronger. He reminds himself of his intrinsic power almost every day, and he never stops learning, acquiring specialty skills and greater knowledge in his field. Imagineering becomes a personal quest – to discover, invent, understand and promote new observations and ideas.

He meticulously plans his forward actions and never hesitates to make the decisions that will help him achieve his goals. Obstacles, roadblocks and even failures are no match for his persistence, and even when he reaches the pinnacle of his success, he never becomes too proud to seek the guidance of wise mentors.

• • • •

"A candle loses nothing
by lighting another candle."
JAMES KELLER
ROMAN PRIEST

• • • •

He continues to be a creator of new concepts, approaches and life. He leads, manages and inspires. He welcomes duty. In return, he gives back to the world. His inner compass is fixed on a course, and in his travels he touches the lives of many, exalting them with distinctive service, kindness, assistance and enlightenment. He is a giver of energy, goodness and positivity. His creativity, talent and charisma are admired near and far.

A sought-after mentor, he shares with others the teachings he received through the books he read, the mentors he sought and his own experiences. As Miguel de Cervantes, considered by many to be the creator of the first modern novel, once noted, "A proverb is a short sentence based on 'looooong' experience."

With a bias toward action, he chooses to explore life's opportunities and become an agent for change. His eloquent communications reverberate with truth, exactitude, logic and direction. He feels pride in what he does, which inspires him to do it even better.

• • • •

> "We make a living by what we get.
> We make a life by what we give."
> **WINSTON CHURCHILL**
> FORMER PRIME MINISTER OF GREAT BRITAIN

• • • •

And he loves – deeply. His Beloved appreciates his passion and rides the waves of fortunes and pitfalls he encounters on the way to his objective. In time, they marry and spawn yet another generation. Life's cycle begins anew.

On the day their first child is born, he lovingly cradles the newborn, offering protection within the confines of his strong arms, just like his Parents once provided him. His eyes mist over as he marvels and ogles at this miracle he helped create, talking amorously in murmurs to the little person who now carries his genes, his surname and his ancestry.

He wonders who this little girl will become. Does she have any superhuman edge? Yes, he thinks to himself. The baby girl is one with him, his Mother and the universe. The girl has the power to be and do anything that germinates, grows and flourishes within the mind. Our Man knows that his responsibility is to give her a solid foundation; the rest will be up to her.

• • • •

> "The maxims of men disclose their hearts."
> **FRENCH PROVERB**

• • • •

He muses on what he will teach her. The intrinsic power of water was a powerful metaphor that spurred our Man to action. He will certainly share this pearl of wisdom with his little princess when the time is right. He will teach her to be a **Washer.**

He will teach her the core values that he has developed, honed and nurtured over time, that have helped him navigate the waters of life – proof positive that success comes from within:

Watch your thoughts; they become words.
Watch your words; they become actions.
Watch your actions; they become habits.

Watch your habits;   they become character.
Watch your character;   it becomes your destiny.

Our Man hopes that his daughter will learn some of life's expensive lessons through imitation and reflection instead of through experience and failures, but knows that she, like him, will have to experience life's hard knocks to grow into the woman he wants her to become. Like his Father before him, our Man wants his children to be better than he is.

• • • •

"Whatever you do, do with all your might."
LATIN PROVERB

• • • •

Our Man's organizational skills help him balance many family responsibilities and his work. At first it is not easy to find time for business trips, school plays and date nights with his Beloved. His competing priorities and responsibilities make for a precarious tightrope, but a close friend and mentor shares the secret for navigating it: It's all about priorities.

In *7 Habits of Highly Effective People*, Stephen Covey offers a table in which readers can compartmentalize daily activities based on their degree of importance and urgency. By concentrating on the top half of the table and consciously setting limits and efficiencies on the lower half, our Man improves his productivity, achievement and balance.

	URGENT	NOT URGENT
IMPORTANT	**Quadrant I** **Time Spent In:** Fire drills, Crises, Deadline-driven projects **Result:** Firefighting *Stress* *Burnout* *Always putting out fires*	**Quadrant II** **Time Spent In:** Self-development, Relationship-building, Envisioning the future, Exercise/recreation **Result:** Quality Time *Happiness* *Personal Growth* *Achieving Goals* *Success*
NOT IMPORTANT	**Quadrant III** **Time Spent In:** Interruptions Unscheduled phone calls Pressing "stuff" **Result:** Distractions *Short-term focus* *Propensity to think goals* *and plans are worthless*	**Quadrant IV** **Time Spent In:** Distractions Busywork Pleasant activities **Result:** Time Wasting *Time occupied by* *non-value-add tasks* *No residual value* *to anyone*

Covey notes that "effective people stay out of Quadrants III and IV because, urgent or not, they aren't important. They also shrink Quadrant I down to size by spending more time in Quadrant II … the heart of effective personal management."

Our Man's calendars have, thus far, been filled with "stuff" – where the world around him dictated his life schedule – rather than what was best and most important and urgent to *him* and his family. He muses over what few but specific things he could do in his personal and professional life that, if repeated on a regular basis, would make the most significant difference. He realizes that sometimes the hardest things to do are the ones that yield the highest returns, the ones that should be done first. Quadrant II activities have that kind of impact. It is clear that his effectiveness takes a quantum leap when he focuses his energy on them. He takes an inventory of what percentage of his time he spends in each quadrant. As he shifts his schedule based on his priorities, he begins to work half-days from home a few times each week so he can spend more time with his family. He begins deferring some tasks until the children are asleep so he can concentrate more effectively on his work and still attend school functions.

As he reads to his children from the books his Parents boxed up from his own childhood, he comes across the Dr. Seuss book they once shared with him, insisting that its message would make a difference in his life. Now it does, in fact, ring true. He just had to discover the truth inside the message, beneath the words.

You have brains in your head.
You have feet in your shoes.
You can steer yourself
Any direction you choose.

He remembers another rhyme his Parents taught him – one that conveys an entirely different meaning to his grown-up self:

When you wish upon a star, makes no difference who you are.
Anything your heart desires will come to you.
If your heart is in your dreams, no request is too extreme.
When you wish upon a star as dreamers do,
Fate is kind, she brings to those who love
The sweet fulfillment of their secret longing.
Like a bolt out of the blue, fate steps in and sees you through.
When you wish upon a star, your dreams come true.

The twinkling diamonds he once gazed upon, hoping for celestial intervention, continue to shine steadfastly, but now he has found that star quality in him; he was a diamond in the rough that needed to be ground and polished.

His wishes fueled the star within, and he stoked the flames with action. Getting a fire started was much easier than extinguishing it.

And then there were the Bible verses he relied on for a while to give him what he wanted without any effort:

> *Ask, and it shall be given you; seek, and ye shall find;*
> *knock, and it shall be opened unto you.*
> *And all things, whatsoever ye shall ask in prayer,*
> *believing, ye shall receive.*

Now he understands that what he asks for in prayerful meditation also requires some action on his part. A truly earnest desire activates our inner compass. That requires listening to the quiet, intangible whispers within the mind – and allowing faith, autosuggestion and our imagination to kick in, activating the beacons of our subconscious mind to help us reach the tangible.

Today, our Man is a dreamer, a contributor, a life force and a sage mentor. He takes intangible energies in the form of ideas, dreams and wishes and transforms them into their physical manifestations. The future begins today!

••••

"If you have built castles in the air, your work
need not be lost; that is where they should be.
Now put the foundations under them."

HENRY DAVID THOREAU
AMERICAN AUTHOR, POET AND NATURALIST

••••

EPILOGUE

Our Man has lived a long and productive life, creating a legacy of improvements to the world in which he lives, yet he is keenly aware that his life will soon draw to a close. After all is said and done, it is the memory of time with his family – full of laughter, play, togetherness, teaching and sharing – that he holds most dear. Laughter itself may seem meaningless, but its effect on the soul is profound. His children, now grown with children of their own, also value these memories more than any trinkets he has bought them over the years.

••••

"Life is lived forward but understood backward."

SOREN KIERKEGAARD
DANISH PHILOSOPHER, THEOLOGIAN AND PSYCHOLOGIST

••••

One sunny summer day, our Man goes to the park with his wife, children and grandchildren to picnic beside the lake. As he sits by the water's edge, covered in blankets that his wife has lovingly wrapped around his neck, her head on his shoulder, both watching the children gleefully splash one another, he muses over his life.

Many moons ago, a Child was born – a Child with an intrinsic power, an inquisitive spirit and a zest for life. His Parents and environment helped enlighten him to many world rhythms. In time he learned of numerous choices available to him. Some he adopted and others he scorned. But he does not re-

••••

"A proverb is not a proverb to you until life illustrates its meaning."

JOHN KEATS
ENGLISH ROMANTIC POET

••••

gret the mistakes and lost time of the past. They helped him realize that the lessons he once heard and considered so glib were truths that made him a stronger, better man – that helped him see that his life has a purpose. In turn, he became a source of inspiration for others and a source of life.

He peers into the water and finds that, after all these years, it still fascinates, inspires, strengthens and rejuvenates him. He leans closer, close enough to see his reflection – and that of his wife, who catches his glance and smiles. That reflected smile – one that beams with love and admiration for him and the life they have built together – fills him with pride for the legacy he will leave. He has taught himself, his children and the many young people he has taken under his wing over the years that a mortal's identity can be defined in one of three ways:

· A life unrealized – **Wisher**;
· A life with halfhearted commitments – **Wishy-Washy**; or
· A life of cleansing, creation, beautification and stewardship
  (ultimate success) – a **Washer**.

He knows that a good teacher teaches the student to teach himself. In the process, he has taught many to make the world a better place by:

Absorbing,
Adapting,
Carrying,
Cleansing,
Creating,
Flowing,
Following,
Forging,
Giving,
Molding
  and shaping,
Nourishing,
Persisting,
Polishing,
Refreshing
  and renewing,
Taming,
Washing and
Working.

In his youth, he read some words that echoed with possibilities but did not ring true:

"We hold these truths to be self-evident, that all men are created equal, that they are endowed by their Creator with certain unalienable Rights, that among these are Life, Liberty and the pursuit of Happiness."

Later in life, he came to understand their significance. He didn't play it safe to settle among the averages. He took calculated risks, albeit experiencing his share of flops and foibles along the way. But pain, he learned, can be a source of strength, just like weight lifting builds muscles, and he remained steadfast in his quest. He created his own future, earning a position among the top 5 percent, the ones who soar with eagles.

••••

"For the whole earth is the tomb of famous men; not only are they commemorated by columns and inscriptions in their own country, but in foreign lands there dwells also an unwritten memorial of them, graven not on stone but in the hearts of men."

PERICLES
GREEK STATESMAN, ORATOR AND GENERAL

••••

This is his legacy, his mark on the world – and that has been enough for this man's life. An ideal world can only be created by ideal people. There is no way to be a perfect man, but there are a million ways to be a good one. **Our Hero** did, in fact, take the road less traveled – and that has made all the difference in the world!

Difficulties have been his lessons, obstacles his challenges and impossibilities his invitations. Our hero is a **Washer.**

So, what difference will *your* difference make?

"When you were born,
you cried and the world rejoiced.
Live your life in such a manner
that when you die,
the world cries and you rejoice."
INDIAN PROVERB

"We will receive not what we idly wish for but what we justly earn. Our rewards will always be in exact proportion to our service."

EARL NIGHTINGALE
MOTIVATIONAL SPEAKER, AUTHOR,
RADIO PERSONALITY AND BUSINESS OWNER

····

PART 2:
MODELS, MOVERS, AND MENTORS

····

"To laugh often and much; to win the respect of intelligent people and the affection of children; to earn the appreciation of honest critics and endure the betrayal of false friends; to appreciate beauty; to find the best in others; to leave the world a bit better, whether by a healthy child, a garden patch or a redeemed social condition; to know that even one life has breathed easier because you lived. This is to have succeeded."

RALPH WALDO EMERSON
AMERICAN PHILOSOPHER AND POET

····

IS THIS JUST A STORY?

You are sure to recognize many individuals in the minuscule sampling of names on the next few pages and in the brief biographies in the following chapters. Heroes in their own right, who came from humble beginnings but found the "silver lining" advantages in their own circumstances.

Some went to college, some dropped out and others never even completed early scholastic education. However, all of them were (or are) highly learned individuals who eagerly pursued life's experiences and teachings.

In time, they drew on their creativity, energy, determination and persistence to build something grander, reaching extraordinary pinnacles of success and benefiting many. Check out their biographies at *www.biography.com* or *en.wikipedia.org*, on their official websites or in your local library.

In your own circles, family and neighborhood, there are many exemplary individuals who have overcome odds of various proportions and have reached noteworthy achievements; others may still be pursuing their dreams. Seek them out and acknowledge their perseverance. Associating with winners breeds a winning mentality.

You know the tremendous effect of actions and thoughts.
Some Desire, others Admire, few Excel!

MEN	Best Known Role(s)
Aristotle	Philosopher and scientist
Benjamin Franklin	U.S. statesman and inventor
Darren T. Kimura	Entrepreneur (Energy Industries)
Edward Moore ("Ted") Kennedy	U.S. senator
Elvis Aaron Presley	Singer and film actor
Frederick Wallace Smith	Businessman (Federal Express)
Harrison Ford	Actor
Henry Ford	Industrialist and inventor
Henry Deutschendorf, Jr. (John Denver)	Singer and songwriter
Jacques-Yves Cousteau	Naval officer and underwater explorer
John Walsh	Television host and victims' rights advocate
Julio Iglesias	Singer and film actor
Ludwig van Beethoven	Composer
Mahatma Gandhi	Peaceful leader
Martin Luther King, Jr.	Civil Rights leader
Melvin "Mel" Brooks Kaminsky	Actor, director and producer
Michael Dell	Businessman (Dell Computers)
Milton Hershey	Manufacturer and philanthropist (Hershey's)
Napoleon Hill	Author and lecturer
Rex David ("Dave") Thomas	Businessman and TV spokesman (Wendy's)
Ronald Wilson Reagan	U.S. statesman and former president
Samuel Moore Walton	Businessman (Walmart)
Scott Scovell Hamilton	Olympic skater
Sir Richard Charles Nicholas Branson	Businessman (Virgin Airlines)
Stephen Edwin King	Author
Steve Irwin	Wildlife expert and TV show host
Steven Paul Jobs	Inventor and entrepreneur (Apple Computers)
Steven Spielberg	Filmmaker, director and producer
Thomas John Watson, Sr.	Businessman (IBM)
Walter Elias Disney	Film animator, producer and businessman
Warren Buffett	Entrepreneur and investor
William ("Bill") Henry Gates	Business pioneer (Microsoft)
William ("Bill") Jefferson Clinton	U.S. statesman and former president

WOMEN	Best Known Role(s)
Agnes Gonxha Bojaxhiu (Mother Teresa)	Missionary
Anne Frank	Diarist
Arianna Huffington	Author and syndicated columnist
Audrey Hepburn	Actress and philanthropist
Billie Jean King	Tennis player
Carlton ("Carly") Sneed Fiorina	Businesswoman (Hewlett-Packard)
Christa McAuliffe	Teacher and astronaut
Christiane Amanpour	International correspondent
Coco Chanel	Fashion designer and businesswoman (Chanel)
Danica Patrick	Racecar driver
Diane Feinstein	U.S. stateswoman
Dolly Parton	Singer, songwriter and actress
Eileen Edwards (Shania Twain)	Singer, songwriter and actress
Florence Nightingale	Hospital reformer
Gloria Steinem	Writer, feminist and social reformer
Helen Keller	Writer and lecturer
Indira Krishnamurthi Nooyi	Businesswoman (Pepsi)
Jeanne ("Goldie") Hawn	Actress, entrepreneur and producer
Joanne ("J.K.") Rowling	Author
Judith Resnik	Engineer and astronaut
Katherine ("Katie") Anne Couric	Television journalist and host
Madeleine Korbel Albright	Former U.S. Sec. of State and U.N. ambassador
Madonna Louise Ciccone	Pop singer
Margaret ("Meg") Cushing Whitman	Businesswoman (eBay)
Margaret Thatcher	British stateswoman, former prime minister
Martha Stewart	Lifestyle guru and businesswoman
Melody Gardot	Musician
Oprah Gail Winfrey	Talk-show host, actress, producer, philanthropist
Peggy Fleming	Olympic skater
Sally Ride	Astronaut and astrophysicist
Sandra Day O'Connor	Former Supreme Court justice
Serena Jameka Williams	Tennis player
St. Joan of Arc	Patriot

FAILURES?

Many times we think that the heroes we have come to admire were born with special privileges or money, or that they were plain lucky – and therefore we, without those advantages, could never achieve the same feats.

But success is measured by your input, or the amount of effort you put forth, *and* your output. Remember, you will have exactly what you intend. If

• • • •

> "If you want to increase your success rate, double your failure rate."
> **THOMAS WATSON, SR.**
> FOUNDER OF IBM

• • • •

you do not succeed quickly and quit, you will get exactly what you intend. If you press on, and keep on pressing on until the finish line, you will get exactly what you intend.

• • • •

> "There are no constraints on the human mind, no walls around the human spirit, no barriers to our progress except those we ourselves erect."
> **RONALD REAGAN**
> 40TH PRESIDENT OF THE U.S.

• • • •

This chapter presents the stories of several "failures" who changed the world.

Watch the videos of
famous "failures" on
www.wisherwasher.com

A BOY NAMED SPARKY
He was a loser who got the last laugh.

For Sparky, school was all but impossible. He failed every subject in the eighth grade and finished high school Physics with a grade of zero. He also flunked Latin, Algebra and English.

He didn't fare much better in sports. Although he managed to make the school's golf team, he promptly lost the only important match of the season. There was a consolation match; he lost that too.

Throughout his youth, Sparky was awkward socially. He was not exactly disliked by other students; no one cared that much. He was astonished if a classmate ever said hello to him outside of school hours. Dating? Hard to say. Sparky never once asked a girl out in high school. He was too afraid of being turned down.

Sparky was a loser. He knew it; his classmates knew it; everyone knew it. So he rolled with it. He made up his mind early in life that if things were meant to work out, they would. Otherwise he would be content with his inevitable mediocrity.

However, one thing was important to Sparky: drawing. He was proud of his artwork. Of course, no one else appreciated it. In his senior year of high school, he submitted some cartoons to the yearbook editors, who rejected them. Still, Sparky was so convinced of his ability that he decided to become a professional artist.

After completing high school, he wrote a letter to Walt Disney Studios. They requested samples of his artwork and suggested the subject of a cartoon they'd like him to create. Sparky spent a great deal of time preparing his submission. Finally the reply came from Disney Studios – rejected! Another loss for the loser.

Unphased, Sparky decided to write his own autobiography in cartoons, the protagonist a little boy loser and chronic underachiever. The results? Anything but rejection. For Sparky, the loser, was Charles Schulz, creator of the *Peanuts* comic strip, and the little cartoon character whose kite would never fly and who never succeeded in kicking a football was Charlie Brown.

Peanuts ran for nearly 50 years, almost without interruption. During the life of the strip, Schulz took only one vacation, a five-week break in late 1997. At its peak, *Peanuts* appeared in more than 2,600 newspapers in 75 countries.

The human spirit knows no bounds; the energy of this individual charges on in our lives and across generations.

SELECT CHARLES SCHULZ QUOTES:

"A whole stack of memories never equal one little hope."

"Don't worry about the world coming to an end today.
It is already tomorrow in Australia."

"If I were given the opportunity to present a gift to the next generation,
it would be the ability for each individual to learn to laugh at himself."

"Sometimes I lie awake at night and ask, 'Where have I gone wrong?'
Then a voice says to me, 'This is going to take more than one night.'"

DOLLY REBECCA PARTON

*She grew up barefooted, wearing hand-me-down
clothes made from scraps; today, the world
knows her name and her music.*

Dolly Parton is the fourth of 12 children born into what she has described as a "dirt poor" family. They lived in a rustic, dilapidated, one-room cabin in Tennessee with no electricity or running water. Four siblings slept in one bed, and all kids worked the fields. The family grew their own food and moved from one shack to another. They never had anything but outdoor toilets. "If you had a two-holer," she once explained, "you were rich." Yet music and her early church experiences would give her the edge she needed to become one of the most-honored female country performers of all time.

By age nine, Parton was performing on local radio and television programs. The day after her high school graduation, she moved to Nashville to continue her career.

In her 30s she was already a successful country singer but felt she had hit a plateau. After years of making the same money and remaining at the same level of artistry, she decided to broaden her musical base from down-home songs to numbers with a hint of rock. "A lot of people thought I had totally lost my mind," she told the Associated Press in 1979. "But I had no fear of change. I expected success, but I was braced for failure. I didn't care if people thought I was wrong. In my own heart, I knew I was doing the right thing."

And boy, was she right! Her words, music and life have resonated with audiences around the world. The Record Industry Association of America has certified 25 of her singles and albums as either Gold Record, Platinum Record or Multi-Platinum Record. She boasts 26 No. 1 hits on the *Billboard* country charts, a record for a female artist. Over the past 40 years, she has created 42 career-top-10 country albums, a record for any artist, and 110 career-charted singles. All-inclusive sales of singles, albums, hits collections, paid digital downloads and compilation usage during Parton's career have reportedly topped 100 million records worldwide.

Despite TV variety shows that lasted only one season and fruitless attempts to secure a solo hit single – a series of "failures" that lasted into the 90s – she could not be discouraged. Today, she is a singer-songwriter, author, multi-instrumentalist, actress, businesswoman and philanthropist. She owns her own theme park (Dollywood) a restaurant chain (Dixie Stampede) and has over 3,000 songs she has written to her credit. Her literacy program, Dolly Parton's Imagination Library, mails one book per month to enrolled children from birth until they enter kindergarten. It has been replicated in 566 counties across 36 U.S. states (as well as in Canada). In December 2007, it expanded to Europe. The program distributes more than 2.5 million free books to children annually.

The human spirit knows no bounds.

SELECT DOLLY PARTON QUOTES:

"I'm not going to limit myself just because people won't accept the fact that I can do something else."

"If you don't like the road you're walking, start paving another one."

"Storms make trees take deeper roots."

"You'll never do a whole lot unless you're brave enough to try."

WALT DISNEY

*He was a farm boy and a high school
dropout who taught the world to dream.*

The man who inspired children and adults worldwide to imagine and seek happier places experienced many, many misfortunes. Yet he persisted doggedly in his quest – and created a company worth billions.

When he was 18 years old, Disney pursued a career drawing political caricatures or comic strips for newspapers, but no one would hire this eager artist. His brother arranged for him to have a short-lived job creating ads for newspapers, magazines and movie theaters. Here, he met his first business partner, Ub Iwerks, with whom he formed Iwerks-Disney Commercial Artists in 1920. The company had problems making ends meet, and by the end of 1922, Disney was living in the office and taking baths once a week at Union Station. In 1923, at age 21, he filed for bankruptcy.

Next, he moved to Los Angeles and paired up with his brother to form what would eventually become the Walt Disney Company. Politics, betrayal and more losses mounted. In 1925 Disney and his wife, Lillian, opted to forgo getting a reliable car so they could get married. Employees abandoned him and went to Universal, his competitor. At age 28, he sold his car for money but refused to relinquish Mickey Mouse, which he created in 1928 with Les Clark and Iwerks. At 31 years old, he had a nervous breakdown – but dusted himself off and pressed on.

Pinocchio, Bambi and *Fantasia* were all considered flops, leaving Disney owing the banks $5 million in 1939. His sales picked up in Europe until World War II broke out and destroyed the market. Hollywood blamed Disney for the studio's misfortunes and said it was because he had "gone highbrow," trying to foist classical music, a wooden puppet and a "dumb deer" on an unwilling public. Bankruptcy loomed again and workers went on strike in the middle of *Dumbo*.

In 1940 he took Walt Disney Productions public, issuing 755,000 shares of stock and saving his studio. When World War II broke out, the U.S. Army took over his Buena Vista studio, throwing out the cameras and audio equipment. He temporarily abandoned production of *Peter Pan, Alice in Wonderland* and *Wind in the Willows*, and by the end of the war was badly in the red. In 1946 he borrowed money from the bank and made *Song of the South*, which won the Oscar for best movie song, "Zip-a-Dee-Doo-Dah."

Despite his partner's insistence that it would be a flop, Disney embarked on the creation of Disneyland, cashing in all of his assets, including his life insurance, to buy the land and hire architects and planners, builders and other contractors. The board and banks all turned Disney down multiple times. But in 1954, in his middle age, he finally got the money he needed to begin construction of Disneyland.

And his tenacity and perseverance finally started paying off in the film business as well. The movie *Mary Poppins*, for example, was borne from a script authored by Pamela Lyndon Travers in 1934. It took Walt Disney 20 years to convince the strong-willed, proprietary and altogether perfectionist Travers to put her signature on the dotted line, which cost Disney 5 percent of the *Mary Poppins* gross profits. Adjusted for inflation, it ranks as No. 23 on the list of all-time box-office earners.

The human spirit knows no bounds.

SELECT WALT DISNEY QUOTES:

"All the adversity I've had in my life, all my troubles and obstacles, have strengthened me … You may not realize it when it happens, but a kick in the teeth may be the best thing in the world for you."

"We keep moving forward, opening new doors and doing new things because we're curious, and curiosity keeps leading us down new paths."

"I have been up against tough competition all my life. I wouldn't know how to get along without it."

"There is great comfort and inspiration in the feeling of close human relationships and its bearing on our mutual fortunes — a powerful force, to overcome the 'tough breaks' which are certain to come to most of us from time to time."

"Get a good idea and stay with it. Do it, and work at it until it's done right."

HENRY FORD

His drive to succeed literally fueled the future of travel.

Henry Ford was the first of William and Mary Ford's six children. He grew up on a prosperous family farm in what is now Dearborn, Michigan. Ford enjoyed a childhood typical of the rural 19th century, spending days in a one-room school and doing farm chores. At an early age, he showed an interest in mechanical things and a dislike for farmwork.

In 1879 16-year-old Ford left home for the nearby city of Detroit to work as an apprentice machinist, occasionally returning to help on the farm. He remained an apprentice for three years before returning to Dearborn. During the next few years, Ford divided his time between operating and repairing steam engines, finding occasional work in a Detroit factory, and overhauling his father's farm implements, as well as lending a reluctant hand with other farmwork. Upon his marriage to Clara Bryant in 1888, Ford supported himself and his wife by running a sawmill.

In 1891 Ford became an engineer with the Edison Illuminating Company in Detroit – a conscious decision to dedicate his life to industrial pursuits. His promotion to chief engineer in 1893 gave him enough time and money to devote attention to his personal experiments on internal combustion engines – experiments that culminated in 1896 with the completion of his own self-propelled vehicle, the Quadricycle. It had four wire wheels that resembled heavy bicycle wheels, was steered with a tiller like a boat and had only two forward speeds and no reverse.

Although Ford was not the first to build a self-propelled vehicle with a gasoline engine, he was one of several automotive pioneers who helped this country become a nation of motorists. In 1899 he started Detroit Automobile Company, which closed soon after its first anniversary. He started the Ford Motor Company at age 40. In 1917 two shareholders, the Dodge brothers, successfully sued Ford. The Dodge brothers, who held 10 percent of Ford's stock at the time and later founded the Dodge brand, claimed that Henry Ford could not keep lowering the price of his cars, yet raising the wages and number of employees. Ford wanted to control the market by boasting low prices, at the cost of revenues and dividends for shareholders. As investors, they wanted money now. In 1919 a court decision forced the Ford Motor

Company to pay a special dividend of $19.275 million, plus interest, to stockholders. That same year, Ford borrowed $75 million from a syndicate of bankers to buy out his remaining stockholders, most importantly the Dodge brothers. By 1923, Ford had 57 percent of the U.S. market share.

The human spirit knows no bounds.

SELECT HENRY FORD QUOTES:

"All Fords are exactly alike, but no two men are just alike. Every new life is a new thing under the sun; there has never been anything just like it before, never will be again. A young man ought to get that idea about himself; he should look for the single spark of individuality that makes him different from other folks and develop that for all he is worth. Society and schools may try to iron it out of him; their tendency is to put it all in the same mold, but I say don't let that spark be lost; it is your only real claim to importance."

"You can't build a reputation on what you are going to do."

"If you think you can do a thing or think you can't do a thing, you're right."

"Anyone who stops learning is old, whether at twenty or eighty. Anyone who keeps learning stays young. The greatest thing in life is to keep your mind young."

"If money is your hope for independence, you will never have it. The only real security that a man will have in this world is a reserve of knowledge, experience and ability."

"You will find men who want to be carried on the shoulders of others, who think that the world owes them a living. They don't seem to see that we must all lift together and pull together."

JACKIE JOYNER-KERSEE
She overcame poverty and tragedy, discrimination and disease,
to become a world-record-holding athlete.

Born into the mean streets of East St. Louis in 1962, she was the second of four children. Her parents married young – her mother age 16 and her father age 14. She was named after Jackie O, because, as her grandmother Jeane Dixon put it, "Someday, this girl will be the first lady of something."

Jackie Joyner did become the first lady of something: track and field. Sports were her way out. "I don't think being an athlete is unfeminine," she once said. "I think of it as a kind of grace."

At age 11, Joyner saw a man gunned down outside her house. A few years later, she spoke to her grandmother on the telephone, only to find out the next day that her grandfather had gotten drunk and shot his wife with a shotgun while she was asleep. There was a liquor store and pool hall across from the Joyner house, which was little more than wallpaper and sticks, with four small bedrooms. "I remember Jackie and me crying together in a back room in that house, swearing that someday we were going to make it," her older brother Al Joyner once said. "Make it out. Make things different."

In high school, Joyner excelled in basketball, volleyball and track and field, as well as in the classroom. After graduating in the top 10 percent of her class of 350, she went west, on scholarship to UCLA, to compete in basketball and track and field.

Jackie Joyner-Kersee was the first woman to register more than 7,000 points in the heptathlon, a demanding seven-event competition that consists of 100-meter hurdles, a high jump, shot put, 200-meter sprints, a long jump, javelin throw and an 800-meter dash – measuring speed, strength and stamina.

After winning the Olympic silver medal in 1984, when she was edged by less than a second for first place, she captured the gold at both the 1988 and 1992 Games. As Bruce Jenner, the 1976 Olympic decathlon champion, once put it, "She's the greatest multi-event athlete ever, man or woman."

"She was shaped by a mother who bound her to excellence," writes Kenny Moore of *Sports Illustrated*, "by an older brother who was an admirer, defender and soul mate, and by a coach who demanded the best use of her gifts and did it so selflessly that she eventually married him."

Often regarded as the best all-around female athlete in the world, Joyner-Kersee has won three Olympic gold medals, one silver and one bronze. At 23 feet, nine inches, she holds the American record for the long jump and the world record for the heptathlon.

In February 2001, 38-year-old Joyner-Kersee made her retirement official. Rather than glancing behind at past triumphs, she seeks new challenges. "It's better to look ahead and prepare," she explained, "than to look back and regret."

The human spirit knows no bounds.

SELECT JACKIE JOYNER-KERSEE QUOTES:

"I think it's the mark of a great player to be confident in tough situations."

"Ask any athlete: We all hurt at times. I'm asking my body to go through seven different tasks. To ask it not to ache would be too much."

"The glory of sport comes from dedication, determination and desire. Achieving success and personal glory in athletics has less to do with wins and losses than it does with learning how to prepare yourself so that at the end of the day, whether on the track or in the office, you know that there was nothing more you could have done to reach your ultimate goal."

"Once I leave this earth, I know I've done something that will continue to help others."

ABRAHAM LINCOLN

He was born to illiterate parents but found freedom in books
– and gave it back to the world tenfold.

Lincoln was born in a one-room log cabin in Kentucky. He lost his mother at age nine and gained a loving stepparent – whom he would refer to as his "angel mother" – a year later.

His early formal education consisted of about 18 months of schooling from itinerant teachers. Both his parents were almost completely illiterate. He once said that, as a boy, he had gone to school "by littles – a little now and a little then." His neighbors later recalled how he would trudge for miles to borrow a book. According to him, however, his early surroundings provided "absolutely nothing to excite ambition for education." Yet this curious and success-driven man needed no *reason* to learn. He educated himself, studying every book he could get his hands on. He mastered *Aesop's Fables*, the Bible, Shakespeare, English history and American history, and developed a plain writing style of his own that puzzled audiences accustomed to more orotund oratory.

In March 1830, the Lincoln family moved to Illinois, young Abraham himself driving the team of oxen. Age 21, six feet four inches tall, he was rawboned and lanky but muscular and physically powerful. He was especially noted for the skill and strength with which he could wield an axe. He spoke with a backwoods twang and walked in the long-striding, flat-footed, cautious manner of a plowman. Good-natured, though somewhat moody, and talented as a mimic and storyteller, he readily attracted friends.

Having no desire to farm, Lincoln tried his hand at a variety of occupations in Illinois. As a rail-splitter, he helped clear and fence his father's new farm. As a flatboatman, he made voyages down the Mississippi River to New Orleans. He worked from time to time as a storekeeper, a postmaster and a surveyor. With the coming of the Black Hawk War (1832), he enlisted as a volunteer and was elected captain of his company. He joked later that he had seen no "live, fighting Indians" during the war but had had "a good many bloody struggles with the mosquitoes." In time, he became a partner in a law firm, a lobbyist and a lawyer.

Among American heroes, Lincoln continues to have a unique appeal for many. This charm derives from his remarkable life story (the rise from humble origins to his dramatic death) and from his distinctively human and humane personality, as well as from his historical role as savior of the Union and emancipator of the slaves. But before this American legend became president of the U.S. at age 51, he:

· Failed in business at 22 years old;
· Lost a legislative election at 23 years old;
· Failed in business again at 24 years old;
· Lost his sweetheart at 26 years old;
· Had a nervous breakdown at 27 years old;
· Was defeated in his run for Speaker at 29 years old;
· Lost his bid for elector at 31 years old;
· Was defeated in his congressional election at 34 years old;
· Was defeated in his bid for senator at 46 years old;
· Lost the vice presidency at 47 years old; and
· Lost another senate race at 49 years old.

The human spirit knows no bounds.

SELECT ABRAHAM LINCOLN QUOTES:

"Every man is said to have his peculiar ambition. Whether it be true or not, I can say for one that I have no other so great as that of being truly esteemed of my fellow men, by rendering myself worthy of their esteem."

"In the end, it's not the years in your life that count. It's the life in your years."

"Most folks are as happy as they make up their minds to be."

"The dogmas of the quiet past are inadequate to the stormy present.
The occasion is piled high with difficulty, and we must rise with the occasion.
As our case is new, so we must think anew and act anew."

"The things I want to know are in books; my best friend
is the man who'll get me a book I ain't read."

"Things may come to those who wait, but only the
things left by those who hustle."

"When I am getting ready to reason with a man, I spend one-third
of my time thinking about myself and what I am going to say
and two-thirds about him and what he is going to say."

HARLAND DAVID ("COLONEL") SANDERS

He was a runaway who didn't succeed until his "retirement."

Sanders was born to a Presbyterian family in Henryville, Indiana. His father, Wilbur David Sanders, died when Harland was five years old, and since his mother worked, he was required to cook for his family. He dropped out of school in seventh grade. When his mother remarried, he ran away from home because his stepfather beat him. During his early years, Sanders worked many jobs, including steamboat pilot, insurance salesman, railroad fireman and farmer. He enlisted in the Army as a private when he was only 16 years old (by lying about his age) and spent his entire service commitment in Cuba. But he didn't find his true calling until many failures – and many years – later.

At age 40, Sanders began cooking chicken dishes and other meals for people who stopped at his service station in Corbin, Kentucky. Since he did not have a restaurant, he served customers in his living quarters. His local popularity grew, and Sanders became a chef at a local motel with a restaurant that seated 142 people. Over the next nine years, he developed his secret chicken recipe and methods.

After the construction of Interstate 75 reduced his restaurant's customer traffic, Sanders was left broke with just one asset – his secret recipe. Sanders, now age 65, used $105 from his first Social Security check to begin franchising Kentucky Fried Chicken (KFC) restaurants.

He kissed his wife good-bye, loaded up his battered old car with his pressure cooker and left his home to visit potential franchisees across the country. He offered his secret chicken recipe to many restaurants for free. It was tough going, and he often slept in his car because there wasn't enough money for a hotel room. All he wanted in return was a small percentage of the sales.

"Get out of here. Who wants a recipe from a white Santa Claus?" the restaurant owners shouted, referring to the dress code Sanders adopted: a white shirt and white trousers. More than 1,000 restaurant owners rejected his offer. On his 1,009th sales visit, one owner finally accepted his offer. Less than 10 years later, Sanders had more than 600 KFC franchises across the U.S. and Canada. Until he was fatally stricken with leukemia in 1980 at the age of 90, the

Colonel traveled 250,000 miles each year to visit KFC restaurants around the world. Kentucky Fried Chicken has grown to become one of the largest quick-food service systems in the world, with more than a billion "finger lickin' good" KFC dinners served annually in more than 80 countries and territories.

The human spirit knows no bounds.

SELECT COLONEL SANDERS QUOTES:

"You got to like your work. You have got to like what you are doing, you have got to be doing something worthwhile so you can like it, because it is worthwhile, that it makes a difference, don't you see?"

"I made a resolve then that I was going to amount to something if I could. And no hours, nor amount of labor, nor amount of money would deter me from giving the best that there was in me. And I have done that ever since, and I win by it. I know."

"There's no reason to be the richest man in the cemetery. You can't do any business from there."

"Feed the poor and get rich or feed the rich and get poor."

SCOTT ADAMS

He became a successful cartoonist because he failed at being an executive.

Born in Windham, New York, in 1957, Adams graduated valedictorian in a class of 39 people. He remained in the area for college, receiving a bachelor's degree in Economics from Hartwick College in 1979. Then he studied economics and management at the University of California, Berkeley, and received an MBA in 1986.

After working 17 years in an unrewarding job, he successfully made the move to cartooning. The transition was not easy, though. To keep his resolution strong and his spirit positive in the face of a multitude of rejections, he wrote, "I will become a syndicated cartoonist" at least 15 times each day. And he kept on sending sample cartoons to syndication services.

Eventually, he did get a syndication contract, but the sales weren't what he'd hoped for. So he talked to his customers, who told him that business humor was the next big thing in comics, and re-focused his work to create a bestseller in *Dilbert*. Since late 2004, his health has created obstacles for his work, but ever perseverant in the face of challenges, he has found creative ways to keep drawing. In 2004 he suffered from a reemergence of focal dystonia, a condition discovered in his youth. Though it has affected his drawing, he works around the problem by drawing using a graphics tablet. He also suffers from spasmodic dysphonia, a condition that causes the vocal cords to behave in an abnormal manner. He recovered from this condition temporarily but, in July 2008, underwent surgery to rewire the nerve connections to his vocal cord. Still, *Dilbert* continues to humor us all!

The human spirit knows no bounds.

SELECT SCOTT ADAMS QUOTES:

"One way to compensate for a tiny brain is to pretend to be dead."

"Creativity is allowing yourself to make mistakes.
Art is knowing which ones to keep."

"You don't have to be a 'person of influence' to be influential.
In fact, the most influential people in my life are probably not
even aware of the things they've taught me."

"There are many methods for predicting the future. For example,
you can read horoscopes, tea leaves, tarot cards or crystal balls.
Collectively, these methods are known as 'nutty methods.' Or you can
put well-researched facts into sophisticated computer models,
more commonly referred to as 'a complete waste of time.'"

"If a job's worth doing, it's too hard."

"Most success springs from an obstacle or failure. I became a cartoonist
largely because I failed in my goal of becoming a successful executive."

"No matter where you are, someone is going to be watching you."

JOANNE ("J.K.") ROWLING

*She created a magical world (and a billion-dollar
enterprise) while living in squalor.*

Rowling was born in England in July 1965, grew up in Chepstow, Gwent, and later attended Exeter University, where she earned degrees in French and Classics. As a postgraduate she moved to London and worked as a researcher at Amnesty International and later as a secretary for several companies. But she was never happy in these roles, and her habit of devising fantasy stories when she should have been working got her fired more than once. "I was never paying much attention in meetings because I was usually scribbling bits of my latest stories in the margins of the pad or thinking up names for my characters," she told BBC News.

The idea for *Harry Potter and the Philosopher's Stone* – the first in the popular series (titled *Harry Potter and the Sorcerer's Stone* for the American release) – came to her during a delayed rail journey between Manchester and London. During the next five years she outlined the plots for each book and began writing the first novel.

When her mother, age 45, died on New Year's Eve in 1990 after a 10-year battle with multiple sclerosis, Rowling's world was rocked. She left the U.K. to teach English in Portugal – where she met her first husband, Portuguese journalist Jorges Arantes – but she continued to write. Rowling gave birth to their daughter, Jessica, in 1993, got divorced soon afterward and moved to Edinburgh to be near her sister.

She initially intended to start teaching again but decided instead to finish her book. "I knew that full-time teaching, with all the marking and lesson planning, let alone a small daughter to care for single-handedly, would leave me with absolutely no spare time at all," she wrote in her website's biography.

Living off welfare payments in "grotty and depressing" government housing, Rowling developed Harry Potter's world as a means of escape. She would wander around the town, pushing Jessica in a baby carriage until the child fell asleep, giving her mother the chance to head for a coffee shop to write. The owners of her favorite cafe, Nicolson's, would let her stay all day, despite the fact that she could only afford to order water and an espresso. And with Jessica sleeping at her side, she wrote out the stories in longhand.

A Scottish Arts Council grant helped her pay for a typewriter, on which she hammered out the manuscript that would eventually convince Bloomsbury Publishing that Potter could be a hit. "I had to type the whole thing out myself. Sometimes I actually hated the book, even while I loved it," Rowling admitted on her official website.

Harry Potter and the Philosopher's Stone hit shelves in the U.K. in 1997 after being rejected by eight publishers. Bloomsbury encouraged her to use initials rather than her name, to keep from alienating the teenage boys who were the target audience for her book. As she had no middle name, Rowling took the "K" from Kathleen, her favorite grandmother.

Since then, the Harry Potter series has sold more than 400 million books in 65 languages worldwide and spawned a series of hit films starring Daniel Radcliffe as the boy wizard. In March 2010, when *Forbes* published its latest list of billionaires worldwide, it estimated Rowling's net worth to be $1 billion. She has become a notable philanthropist, supporting such charities as Comic Relief, One Parent Families, Multiple Sclerosis Society of Great Britain and the Children's High Level Group.

The human spirit knows no bounds.

SELECT J.K. ROWLING QUOTES:

*"Differences of habit and language are nothing at all
if our aims are identical and our hearts are open."*

"It matters not what someone is born, but what they grow to be."

*"Destiny is a name often given in retrospect to choices
that had dramatic consequences."*

"You sort of start thinking anything's possible if you've got enough nerve."

IMPAIRED?

••••

"The only disability in life is a bad attitude."
SCOTT HAMILTON
AMERICAN FIGURE SKATER AND OLYMPIC GOLD MEDALIST

••••

Life bestows upon each of us certain gifts and challenges. Some of these burdens we are born with (such as chronic illness or deformity) and others are thrust upon us in the most unexpected ways (such as death, divorce or financial troubles). Yet, even in the throes of setback we can find the nuggets of wisdom that will set us apart from everyone else. We can use the stones we find in the wreckage as building blocks for future glory.

Seek out the many winners who have overcome physical, mental or emotional impairments and you will invariably hear that they believe these hurdles have given them an edge. They have reached the pinnacles of success because they had to try harder than everyone else – and that made all the difference.

In the following pages, you will read the stories of just a few of these inspirational individuals who persevered in the face of obstacles that would have caused the average person to give up.

JAMES EARL JONES

He became the voice everyone recognizes after eight years of silence.

The only child of Robert Earl and Ruth Connolly Jones, James Earl Jones was born on January 17, 1931, in Arkabutla, Mississippi. Before his son's birth, James's father left the family to pursue a career as a boxer and later as an actor. Ruth Jones left soon after to find work, leaving her separated from her son for long periods of time. At age five, Jones, a Black Indian, was adopted by his maternal grandparents – an ex-slave and a former indentured servant. This was during the Great Depression, a slowdown in the country's system of producing, distributing and using goods and services that caused millions of Americans to lose their jobs. Jones told *Newsweek* that being abandoned hurt him deeply. "No matter how old the character I play," he said, "those deep childhood memories, those furies, will come out. I understand this."

Eventually Jones's grandparents took him north to Michigan, where he struggled in his new surroundings. He developed a stutter and soon found communication so difficult that, at certain periods during grammar school, he could talk only to himself or his immediate family. As James once put it, "One of the hardest things in life is having words in your heart that you can't utter."

He was functionally mute for eight years, until he reached high school, where, determined to overcome his affliction, he recited a poem in class every day, and an English teacher suggested he memorize speeches and enter speaking contests.

Jones attended the University of Michigan on a full scholarship intending to study medicine and take acting classes as a hobby. But in his electives, he found his passion and soon switched his major to theater. When he was 21 years old and a junior at Michigan, he traveled to New York City to meet his father for the first time. The relationship was strained by the many years they had been apart, but Jones's father encouraged him to pursue his passion.

Jones graduated from Michigan in 1953 with a bachelor's degree in drama but joined the army straightaway. He was set to reenlist in 1955 when his commanding officer suggested that he take a break before making a long-term commitment. Jones moved to New York City and lived with his father while he took more acting classes and earned extra money by polishing theater floors. In 1957 the younger Jones earned his first professional role in a production of *Wedding in Japan*. Although he was rarely out of work after that, his salary during the late 1950s averaged only $45 a week.

He went on to become an award-winning television, stage and screen actor, known for his voice-overs as well as for his most famous role, Darth Vader in the *Star Wars* films.

The human spirit knows no bounds.

MELODY GARDOT

She transformed a tragic debilitating accident into musical genius that resonates in the heart.

At age 19, Melody Gardot suffered a horrific accident that nearly killed her. While riding her bike through Philly to the college where she was studying fashion, she was struck by an SUV driver who made an illegal turn and rammed into her. The crash left her with shattered bones (including a fractured pelvis and damaged spine) and severe neurological damage (including memory loss, problems with speech and a hypersensitivity to light and sound). In her own words, she was "a bit of a vegetable." But instead of mourning over lemons, she made lemonade.

The prognosis was not good. Dr. Richard Jermyn, a specialist at the University of Medicine and Dentistry of New Jersey, didn't think she would recover but didn't give up hope. "Your brain is like a computer," he explained to her. "And your computer's still intact. Your hardware, your memory, it's there. You can't access it." When therapy and drugs failed to improve her condition, Dr. Jermyn suggested Gardot, who had played piano in college, try music.

Now a world-renowned jazz artist, Gardot turned to music to help rebuild cognitive function, struggling against drastic short-term memory loss to remember the briefest pattern of notes, strumming a guitar while lying on her back to keep the pain at bay. She sings about the experience soberly and elegantly in "Some Lessons," the first song that came to her during this period of downtime and recovery that she used to hone her talent: *"Remember the sound of the pavement, world turned upside down / City streets unlined and empty, not a soul around ... Some lessons we learn the hard way."*

Gardot never gave up. It took years, but the music therapy slowly began to re-build the neural pathways in her brain – and gave her a new calling. When her songs were posted on MySpace in 2006, her popularity spread like wildfire.

"To be honest with you, being on stage and performing is the 30, 40, 50 minutes of the most pleasurable experience that I have," Gardot told National Public Radio in a 2008 interview. "Because it's during that time that I don't really feel any pain. I think it's transcendental, and I also think it's kind of like when you have a headache, and someone punches you in the stomach, you forget all about your head." She hasn't forgotten about her good fortune, though. "I forget a lot of things, but I don't forget that."

She still has to wear dark glasses because of her sensitivity to light, and she carries a cane to counter occasional attacks of vertigo.

Her experiences only add poignancy, intended or otherwise, to the themes of regret, acceptance and elusive love that inhabit Gardot's self-penned lyrics. "I would be lucky to find me a man who could love me the way that I am," she sings on one of her title tracks.

Gardot continues to build on what her self-made luck has wrought – the un-likely fruit of those bed-ridden days spent plucking and humming just to re-build her cognition and stay sane. Today, Melody Gardot is an American jazz singer, writer and musician. Her CDs are sold worldwide.

Gardot often speaks about the benefits of music for therapy and pain man-agement. She has visited various universities and hospitals to speak about its ability to help reconnect neural pathways in the brain, improve speech abil-ity and lift patients' spirits.

The human spirit knows no bounds.

STEVLAND HARDAWAY JUDKINS ("STEVIE WONDER")

He was blind but he could see – his own potential to rock the world.

Blind from infancy, Wonder took up piano at age seven – and mastered it by age nine. The boy, who was very active in his church choir, also taught himself to play the harmonica and drum, mastering both by age 10. At age 13, he scored his first major hit, "fingertips (Pt. 2)." In 1973 a serious automobile accident left him in a coma for four days and permanently without yet another of his primary senses: his smell. Undaunted, he went on to become a singer-songwriter/producer who recorded more than 30 top-10 hits and won 26 Grammy Awards. In 2009 he was named a U.N. Messenger of Peace.

Wonder credits much of his success to a teacher in Detroit who helped him recognize for the first time how his blindness could be an asset. She asked him to help her find a mouse that was lost in the classroom. To his amazement, she explained that he was the most qualified student to find it because nature had given him something no one else in the room had: a remarkable pair of ears to compensate for his blind eyes. This was really the first time someone had shown appreciation for those talented ears, he explained many years later, and the beginning of a new life for him. From that time on, he developed his gift of hearing and went on to become one of the greatest pop singers and song-writers of our time.

The human spirit knows no bounds; the energy of this individual charges on in our lives, and across generations.

••••

"Many of life's failures are people who did not realize how close they were to success when they gave up."

THOMAS EDISON
AMERICAN INVENTOR, SCIENTIST AND BUSINESSMAN

••••

Visit www.wisherwasher.com for videos and other stories of real-life "failures" of all ages.

PART 3:
YOUR TURN

PERSONAL ROADMAP

Arriving safely at your destination is a lot easier when you've got a map. You can see the starting point, some of the twists and turns, rest-stops along the way and your final destination. Without a good map or reliable GPS system, even those among us with an impeccable sense of direction run the risk of getting seriously off-course when the journey is as long and arduous as the journey of life can be.

In the following pages, you will have an opportunity to use the ideas, principles and philosophies we've covered in the book thus far to create your own personal roadmap. It is the navigational chart for your life's adventure, a map that will help you plan your own odyssey – one that will be unique to you alone.

You will begin with a very big picture of where you are now, marking some of the things that you want to add into your personal quiver as you journey towards your purpose. Next comes the opportunity to reflect on who you really are, and who you really want to become. Then you'll set your priorities to help you structure your time and goals so that you can structure your future.

And last but not least, you will have the opportunity to make a commitment to yourself (the most important person on this planet) – to create the change, and the magic, that you want in your life, and to find your purpose. Remember, you alone are in charge of your destiny!

MY PERSONAL ODYSSEY

On the following page is a personal odyssey roadmap that you can create for yourself. Circle all of the elements you would like to experience but have not, or that you want to experience more of, and then draw a line starting with the "status quo," interconnecting each of these circles in the order that you feel is best for you, until you end up in "self-transcendence." Annotate by what year you would like to have accomplished each task next to the circle.

This is a journey that will take years to accomplish, but it will be much easier once you have your roadmap in place, methodically guiding you to each destination. Each person will traverse it differently, with lines criss-crossing up and down and to and fro, but *this* will be the journey that *you* want to take. In this odyssey, obstacles, grief, conflict resolution, setbacks and even failure will be part-and-parcel – as will laughter, play, relaxation, dreams, fantasies, learning, sacrifice and reflection. It means relinquishing old hates and grievances along the way, burdens you may be clinging to as if they were treasures. But in reality, they will only blind you to the richness of life. Some of the items on the map, once started and experienced, will become a standard in your life. It is how you will navigate your personal success.

I encourage you to connect all of the points in your own style and then revel in the enlightenment as you pursue your own realizations, training and levels of refined polishing. Crossing all points will mark personal and business excellence.

Before you get started, consider this: where is your attitude on the Attitude Meter? This will determine what types of goals you set. If you're feeling positive, enthusiastic and energetic when you approach personal development and *goal-setting*, your outcome will be greater. If you're feeling more glass-half-empty at the moment, your results will reflect that negative energy.

Ready, set ... go!

Attitude Meter

Negative   Neutral   Positive

SELF-
ACTUALIZATION

Forgiveness

Safety   Financial Security

Cultural
Expansion

Experience   Personal Reflection

                                                SMART Goals

                        Travel   Leadership

Children   Life Contribution

                Esteem Needs   Education

Giving   Positive Attitude Development

Personal Learning
and Reading   Purpose

Career Change   Family

                Training   Promotion
                                Opportunities

Team Development   Belongingness

            Faith   Extra-Curricular Activities

Cultural
Orientation   Customers

                            Innovation

                Merits

Community Service   Aesthetic Needs

            Self Reflection

Home   Restitution   Development
                                                of a Successor
            Mentorship

Teaching   Support Groups

                Need to Know
                and Understand

                                    More Education

Career Development

                            Excitement for
                            Differences
                            and Similarities

                Love
                                    Physical Self-Development

STATUS
QUO

MY REFLECTIONS

Reflect on the questions below and write down your answers. This is a time-consuming activity, but if you invest in your life planning, you *will* reap the rewards!

1. What activities, dialogues or desires resonate with me?

2. What sacrifices and commitments am I ready to make? What am I willing to give up so that I may gain in the long run?

3. How much personal time will I devote each day to strengthening my mind? What books, audio programs and biographical clips will I leverage to quickly learn what others have experienced before me?

4. What character virtues do I want to build, and how will I do this? (Use the list on page 68 for inspiration.)

5. What is weighing me down, keeping me from soaring to new heights?

6. What gripes, disappointments and hatred am I carrying around like a hot coal in my hand, waiting to hurl at someone? I must let it go, as I am the one getting burned. How will I forgive and move on?

7. Am I giving back to my family and community?
Am I paying it forward with my deeds? How?

8. Am I giving mindless rhetoric or mindful delivery?
How will I improve?

9. What multiple streams of opportunity can I pursue?

10. Am I just "talking the talk," or am I "walking the talk"?
What can I do to live what I dream and practice what I preach?

11. Who are my mentors? Who do I want to be like? How can I emulate them? What will I do to be in their company? What will I do to learn about them on a daily, weekly or monthly basis?

12. In order to get great customer service in my life, am I being a good customer? After all, the world will reflect back to me what I project. What habits do I need to cultivate?

13. What will I do daily to achieve my goals
and how will I apply a DWIT attitude?

14. The company owns the job; I own my career!
What will I do to further my career and help my company?

15. What would I like to DO? What is my purpose?

MY PLAN

First things first – what are my priorities?
Where am I spending my precious time?

	URGENT	NOT URGENT
IMPORTANT		
NOT IMPORTANT		

GOAL SETTING

This is the exciting part – where your wishful thinking gets committed to paper so it can be put into practice. It is where you become accountable to yourself for *doing* the things you want to do, the things you've been *wishing* and "planning" to do. This is not about what anyone else wants for you. *You* are planning your future today.

••••

> "It is a simple task to make things complex,
> but a complex task to make things simple."
> **CHINESE PROVERB**

••••

This goal-setting exercise follows the SMART principle – allowing you to set a date for when you will accomplish each goal and then measure your progress.

S *pecific:*   Goals are defined by explicit results or outcomes, such as "I will obtain a SCUBA certification" or "I will complete an accounting course."

M *easurable:*   Goals include clear metrics, such as "I will have the certificate in my hand" or "I will get a B or better in the course."

A *chievable:*   Goals are reachable with your current physical, mental and emotional abilities – though they may require that you stretch yourself.

R *esource Based:*   Goals are reachable with your current resources, including time and money.

T *ime Based:*   Goals are assigned specific dates for start and completion, such as "I will lose 20 pounds in three months."

If you earnestly work to accomplish the goal but fall short, you will still be able to sleep well at night because you gave it your best shot and are much farther along than if you had never started. The day after, you can begin anew.

• • • •

"If you would hit the mark, you must aim a little above it; every arrow that flies feels the attraction of earth."

HENRY WADSWORTH LONGFELLOW
AMERICAN EDUCATOR AND POET

• • • •

Break your goals into categories using the charts on the following pages, and don't list so many that you cannot accomplish them. Some may take a year to accomplish, others five and others more than a decade. Below is a list of examples for each category. This is merely for clarification and inspiration. Your goals are your own.

FUN: WHAT HOBBIES OR ADVENTURES WILL YOU PURSUE?

Examples: Go to Disneyland, visit Athens, climb Kilimanjaro, learn to golf or paint, fly a plane, go horse-back riding, adopt a dog, let your hair grow out or snorkel in the Caribbean.

PERSONAL DEVELOPMENT: WHAT WILL YOU READ, LEARN, EXPERIENCE OR *DO* TO GROW?

Examples: Take a particular class, attend a choice seminar, read a specific book, subscribe to magazines of interest, travel to a new place or contribute time to those in need.

CAREER: HOW WILL YOU FOLLOW YOUR PURPOSE AND PASSION AT WORK?

Examples: Pursue certification or a degree that aligns with my purpose or makes me better at my job, start a business or have a family (children *are* a full-time job).

FINANCIAL: HOW WILL YOU MAKE YOURSELF MORE FINANCIALLY SECURE?

Examples: Pay off a certain debt, increment savings by X amount or establish credit to buy a house.

HEALTH: WHAT WILL YOU DO TO IMPROVE YOUR OVERALL HEALTH?

Examples: Work out three days a week, lose 20 pounds, quit smoking or eat more vegetables.

RELATIONSHIPS: HOW WILL YOU STRENGTHEN THE RELATIONSHIPS THAT MEAN THE MOST TO YOU?

Examples: Visit my grandmother, have a weekly date night with my spouse, take my kids to the park to fly kites every couple weeks or schedule an outing with a close friend I don't see often.

WHAT ARE YOUR SHORT-TERM
(ONE-YEAR) GOALS?

Category	#	Description	Plan of Action (strategy)	Accomplished (at end of year)?
FUN				O YES O NO
				O YES O NO
				O YES O NO
PERSONAL DEVELOPMENT				O YES O NO
				O YES O NO
CAREER				O YES O NO
				O YES O NO
FINANCIAL				O YES O NO
				O YES O NO
HEALTH				O YES O NO
				O YES O NO
RELATIONSHIPS				O YES O NO
				O YES O NO
				O YES O NO
EVALUATION DATE				

Be bold; dream big! List all items you want to experience. In five years, what positions, travels, relationships, income, house and car do you want to have?

Category	#	Description	Plan of Action (strategy)	Accomplished (at end of year)?
FUN				O YES O NO
				O YES O NO
				O YES O NO
PERSONAL DEVELOPMENT				O YES O NO
				O YES O NO
CAREER				O YES O NO
				O YES O NO
FINANCIAL				O YES O NO
				O YES O NO
HEALTH				O YES O NO
				O YES O NO
RELATIONSHIPS				O YES O NO
				O YES O NO
				O YES O NO
EVALUATION DATE				

WHAT IS YOUR
TEN-YEAR PLAN?

Category	#	Description	Plan of Action (strategy)	Accomplished (at end of year)?
FUN				O YES O NO
				O YES O NO
				O YES O NO
PERSONAL DEVELOPMENT				O YES O NO
				O YES O NO
CAREER				O YES O NO
				O YES O NO
FINANCIAL				O YES O NO
				O YES O NO
HEALTH				O YES O NO
				O YES O NO
RELATIONSHIPS				O YES O NO
				O YES O NO
				O YES O NO
EVALUATION DATE				

MY SUCCESS FORMULA

Ready to calculate your own success formula? Review the formula illustrated in the story and then use the questions that follow to get you started. Visit *wisherwasher.com* for help in doing the math by clicking on the formula tab.

$$\frac{\text{Success}}{\text{Potential}} = \frac{5\% \text{ who succeed}}{X} \left[\frac{\left[\text{Innate Attributes} + \text{Acquired Attributes}\right] \times \text{Technology} \times \text{Mental Attitude} \times \text{People You Know}}{\frac{\text{Number of Tries} - \text{Number of Failures}}{\text{Number of Tries}}} \right]$$

S_P = **Success Potential:** number of people who will reap *my benefits*

IA = **Innate Attributes:** advantages I was born with, such as health, speed, dexterity and memory

AA = **Acquired Attributes:** skills I have learned, been trained in and polished – such as my technical education, degree or specialized experience

T = **Technology:** my proficiency and application of such things as text messaging, standardized manufacturing procedures, international standards, e-mail, high-speed Internet, social networking, computers or new equipment, or software

NT = **Number of Tries Before Success**

NF = **Number of Failures Experienced** (always expressed as NT or NT-1)

MA = **Mental Attitude** (factors range from -1 to +1, as illustrated in the next chart)

P = **People:** those I know who can directly benefit from my product/service

• • • •

"Ask for the impossible; obtain the best possible."

ENRIQUE RUIZ

• • • •

YOUR TURN

Before you calculate your own success formula,
consider the questions below.

What are my IAs? What am I naturally good at?

**What are my AAs? What training, education and experiences
have I acquired? What AAs do I still need to acquire to achieve
the acclaim I deserve? How will I set out to get this experience?**

What technological skills (T) have I learned that can I use to reach my goals? What do I need to learn to improve in this area?

How many NTs, NFs and modifications am I willing to endure?

How is my MA, and what will I DO to get it where it needs to be?

What actions can I add to my daily routine to improve my MA?

How is my dress affecting my attitude? Am I dressing
with intent? What impression am I leaving behind?

Are the seeds and nourishment I implant in my mind
growing weeds that crowd out my thoughts, or are they
leads for my dreams? How can I improve?

Are my mind, brain and body in sync with my attitude?
Since body language is the unspoken truth, what are my
countenance and posture telling others?

How can I expand my circle of influence and know more people
(P)? Am I building the rapport I need with the right people who
can help me and take me under their wings? How will I adjust my
time and behavior to build quality rapport with the right people?

What does my success formula reveal about my success potential?

(Use your answers to calculate your success formula at wisherwasher.com.)

· · · ·

"Try to remember that a dedicated teacher
is a valuable messenger from the past,
and can be an escort to your future."
ALBERT EINSTEIN
THEORETICAL PHYSICIST AND PHILOSOPHER

· · · ·

MY COMMITMENT

I promise to keep the commitments I have made to myself above, recognizing that I have to be true to myself before I can expect to give (or receive) anything from others.

_____   _____

DATE   SIGNATURE

Witnessed by: _____

Someone you trust to hold you accountable

Happy are those who dream dreams and ...
are ready to pay the price to make them come true!

••••

"All men dream, but not equally. Those who dream by night in the dusty recesses of their minds wake in the day to find that it was vanity: but the dreamers of the day are dangerous men, for they may act their dream with open eyes, to make it possible."

T. E. LAWRENCE
BRITISH ARMY OFFICER DEPICTED IN THE MOVIE _LAWRENCE OF ARABIA_

••••

INDIVIDUALITY

ENCOURAGEMENT

SYNERGY

TALENT

D DETERMINATION

I

V VALUE

E

R RESPECT

S

I INCLUSION

T

Y YOU

SOURCES FOR PART 1: THE STORY

Allen, Robert G. and Mark Victor Hansen. *The One Minute Millionaire.* Harmony Books, 2002. (http://snipurl.com/1minute)

Bachelder, Louise and Jeff Hill. *Abraham Lincoln: Wisdom and Wit.* Peter Pauper Press, 1965.

Cady, Barbara and Jean-Jacques Naudet. *They Changed The World: 200 Icons Who Have Made a Difference.* Tess Press, 2003. (http://snipurl.com/200icons)

Calaprice, Alice. *The New Quotable Einstein.* Princeton University Press, 2005.

Chapman, Gary. *The five Love Languages.* Northfield Publishing, 1995. (http://snipurl.com/fivelove)

Covey, Stephen. *The Seven Habits of Highly Effective Families: Building a Beautiful Family Culture in a Turbulent World.* Golden Books Publishing, 1997. (http://snipurl.com/7familyhabits)

Covey, Stephen. *The Seven Habits of Highly Effective People.* Simon and Schuster, 2004. (http://snipurl.com/7effectivehabits)

Elffers, Joost and Gary Goldschneider. *The Secret Language of Birthdays: Personology Profiles for Each Day of the Year.* Harper Collins, 1994. (http://snipurl.com/birthdaylanguage)

Geary, James. *The World in a Phrase: A Brief History of the Aphorism.* Bloomsbury Publishing, 2005.

Hill, Napoleon. *Think & Grow Rich.* Ballantine Publishing Group, 1960. (http://snipurl.com/richthought)

Maxwell, John C. *Talent Is Never Enough.* Thomas Nelson Publishing, 2007. (http://snipurl.com/talent2)

Mourkogiannis, Nikos. Purpose: *The Starting Point of Great Companies.* Palgrave Macmillan, 2006. (http://snipurl.com/inspire)

Nightingale, Earl. *Lead the field.* Nightingale Conant, 1990. (http://snipurl.com/leadfield)

Phillips, Bob. *Book of Great Thoughts and Funny Sayings.* Tyndale House Publishers,1993.

Pilzer, Paul Zane. *The Next Millionaires.* ZCI, 2007. (http://snipurl.com/nextmillion)

Schwartz, David J., Ph.D. *The Magic of Thinking Big.* Simon & Schuster, 1965. (http://snipurl.com/magicthink)

Secretan, Lance H.K. *Inspire: What Great Leaders Do.* John Wiley & Sons, 2004. (http://snipurl.com/inspire)

Souza, Brian. *Become Who You Were Born to Be.* Paragon Holdings, 2005. (http://snipurl.com/borntobe)

Tracy, Brian. *The Psychology of Achievement.* The Nightingale Conant, 1987.

Tsika, Paul E. *Sequoia-Size Success: Unlocking Your Potential For Greatness.* Plow On Publications, 2005.

SOURCES FOR PART 2: MODELS, MOVERS AND MENTORS

CHARLES SCHULZ BIOGRAPHY

Nightingale, Earl. *"A Boy Named Sparky."* Bits & Pieces.
Vol. T/No. 15. The Economic Press, 1998.

DOLLY PARTON BIOGRAPHY

Thomas, Bob. *"Dolly Parton Expected Success But Understood Risk of Failure."* Schenectady Gazette. 1979. <http://www.dailygazette.com/google_search/ ?=dolly%20parton%20bob%20thomas>

WALT DISNEY BIOGRAPHY

Mosley, Leonard. *Disney's World: A Biography.* Scarborough House,1990.

HENRY FORD BIOGRAPHY

flink, James J. *"Henry Ford."* American National Biography. 2000.
<http://www.taftcollege.edu/newtc/Academic/INCO48/sec4-anb_ford.htm>

"The Life of Henry Ford." The Henry Ford Museum
<http://www.hfmgv.org/exhibits>

Mourkogiannis, Nikos. *Purpose: The Starting Point of Great Companies.*
Palgrave Macmillan, 2006. (http://snipurl.com/inspire)

JACKEE JOYNER-KERSEE BIOGRAPHY

"Jackee Joyner-Kersee Biography." The Biggest Stars.
<http://www.biggeststars.com/j/jackie-joyner-kersee-biography.html>.

ABRAHAM LINCOLN BIOGRAPHY

Ishola, Ibukunolu. *"Persistence."* Food for Thought Blog.
<http://ibukunoluishola.blogspot.com/2007/04/persistence.html>.

Current, Richard N. *"Abraham Lincoln Biography."* Biography.com.
<http://www.biography.com/articles/Abraham-Lincoln-9382540>.

WILLIAM DAVID "COLONEL" SANDERS BIOGRAPHY

"Colonel Harland Sanders: From Young Cook to KFC's Famous Colonel."
Kentucky Fried Chicken. 2000. <http://www.kfc.com/about/colonel.asp>

SCOTT ADAMS BIOGRAPHY

"Leadership…with a human touch." Economics Press. New Jersey, May 2002.

J.K. ROWLING BIOGRAPHY

"Everything You Might Want to Know." J.K. Rowling Official Site. <http://www.jkrowling.com/textonly/en/>.

"J.K. Rowling: From Rags to Riches." BBC News. 2008. <http://news.bbc.co.uk/2/hi/uk_news/politics/7626896.stm>.

JAMES EARL JONES BIOGRAPHY

"James Earl Jones." Encyclopedia of Word Biography. <http://www.notablebiographies.com/Jo-Ki/Jones-James-Earl.html>.

MELODY GARDOT BIOGRAPHY

"How Melody Gardot Found Her Voice." CBS News. 2010. <http://www.cbsnews.com/stories/2010/01/24/sunday/main 6136473.shtml>

"Melody Gardot's Road to Recovery." NPR. 2008. <http://www.npr.org/templates/story/story.php?storyId=87997628.>

Mitter, Siddhartha. *"Beginning Her Career Purely By Accident."* Boston Globe. 2008. <http://www.boston.com/ae/music/articles/2008/08/08/beginning_her_career_purely_by_accident/>.

STEVIE WONDER BIOGRAPHY

Carnegie, Dale. *How to Win Friends and Influence People.* Pocket Books, 1981. (http://snipurl.com/winpeople)

QUOTATIONS

Many of the famous quotations throughout the book were also listed on such sites as quotationspage.com, quotedb.com and quotecosmos.com.

Please note that Internet links can change over time, but those listed here are accurate as of the date of publication.

*For other books and resources about life,
visit www.positivepsyche.biz*

ABOUT THE AUTHOR

I served as the Deputy Program Mgr on a billion-dollar program for a Fortune 100 company, managing a nation-wide operation with a workforce that was 15,000 strong. This was my plateau of success at the moment. How did a once-homeless person who lived in the back of his truck in a homemade camper make it here?

I floundered in school at an early age. Over time, I learned to appreciate the value of learning. My work ethic improved, and as I built my career, several individuals took me under their wings, giving me new insights into leadership. I earned this reward by working hard to contribute to the success of my superiors and teammates. Through the Law of Reciprocity, I gained more experiences and benefits.

My profession, however, has not run a straight and narrow course. I have taken many twists and turns along the way. Different companies and a wide range of varied roles and positions define my career – as do many business ventures peppered in along the way. Today, I am also a writer and an inventor.

I have lived in the U.K. and in Mexico, and across the U.S. I am very fortunate to grow and experience the seasons of life with a loving and united family. Together, we look forward to riding the waves of existence and potentiality affecting new paradigm changes, as Washers. I am most thankful to my wife Sarah, our children Molly, Hannah, Shaun, Shaina and Sasha (in remembrance), and our new son-in-law George for the laughter, the bonds, the work ethic, the passion and the opportunity to help each other make a difference in the world.

It is my desire that you will find in this fictional story (in which many of the experiences and success formulas are real) a spark that will ignite your passion to excel, contribute and succeed.

BOOK **ENRIQUE RUIZ** TO SPEAK AT YOUR
NEXT SCHOOL, CONFERENCE OR CORPORATE EVENT
Those who can see through the visible can achieve the impossible!

Looking for the perfect keynote speaker or presenter for your next conference, workshop, leadership training program or other corporate event? Let Enrique Ruiz empower and inspire your audience with his trademark presentations:

Tapping into the Silent Murmurs of Your Organization

Diversity appreciation is powerful. Numerous studies have shown that when companies and leaders really focus on it (not just pay it lip-service), diversity can make a huge impact on not only morale, but also on the bottom line! So, how do you truly diversify – beyond quotas and policies – and effectively build an inclusive workforce? You uncover the diamonds within your organization by tapping into the quiet murmur of thoughts in each and every employee.

The Power of Transformation: Diversity and Me

Each individual has a unique history – one that includes experiences, culture, faith, family, survival and education – and so each of us has a completely unique vantage point. These differing perspectives, if properly and fully tapped, can offer a tremendous competitive advantage to organizations. By understanding how people from different backgrounds tick, and fostering a culture where everyone feels respected, accepted and appreciated, you can create a stronger, more productive and engaged workforce – which will boost morale, innovation *and* revenue!

A History of Discrimination, and How
to Change Your Own Discriminating Behavior

Because we cannot fully understand the present and effectively mold the future without understanding our pasts and ourselves, Enrique examines the history of discrimination and answers all the questions about other races and religions most of us are afraid to ask for fear of seeming racist or ignorant. Even more importantly, audience members will begin to recognize their own hidden biases and prejudices – and begin to better understand and appreciate, as well as communicate and collaborate with, individuals from different backgrounds – so they can build bridges of trust that propel their companies forward in our increasingly competitive (and increasingly global) economy.

Wisher to Washer: How to Move from Just Existing to Personal Abundance

Imagine the future that you want. Is it different from where you are now? Do you think you have what it takes to be successful? Are you a leader with vision, values, mission and purpose? Are you equipped with the ingredients necessary to create the life you want to live? There are three types of people – *Wishers*, *Washers* and *Wishy-Washys*. Most wish, some flounder and few excel. Find out how you can move from just existing, to personal abundance!

TO BOOK ENRIQUE FOR YOUR NEXT EVENT, CALL **800.460.8013**
www.americasdiversityleader.com/speaking.php

Wisher, Washer, Wishy-Washy:
How to Move From Just Existing to Personal Abundance

Imagine the future that you want. Is it different from where you are now? Do you think you have what it takes to be successful? Are you a leader with vision, values, mission and purpose? Are you equipped with the ingredients necessary to create the life you want to live? Why does only 5 percent of the population attain phenomenal success while many others lead lives of quiet desperation? Is it luck? Genes? Age? Environment? Nope. Most people dream of success but, as they grow older, settle into believing that life got in the way, that their unfulfilled dreams and unachieved goals were simply not meant to be. Not true. It is a matter of choice and of persistence, coupled with dogged determination in the face of obstacles, setbacks and failures. Success, when you've scaled the mountain and really earned it, is so much sweeter. And wishing for success and committing yourself to it are two very different things. So, are you a *Wisher* or a *Washer*, or just plain *Wishy-Washy?*

www.wisherwasher.com

The "W" Characters: How to Get What You Want AND Make a Difference in the World

Children understand far more than most adults give them credit for. As a society, we teach children how to do things and the difference between right and wrong. We answer their questions (as much as possible) about what and why things are. But children are also capable of understanding much deeper life principles – like the importance of building character, how to make decisions, the consequences of relying on others to make their dreams come true and the value of their word. In this story of a group of children who gather for an overnight camping trip that changes their young lives, *The "W" Characters* gets these messages across in a fun, easy-to-read presentation that they'll want to read again and again.

www.characterforchildren.com

Lost Love: 365+ Ways Couples Grow Apart Without
Realizing it and How to Reclaim Your Closeness

Isn't falling in love grand – the butterflies, the passion, the best behavior, the promise of a shining future? But we are not perfect people and we do not lead blissfully perfect, fairy-tale lives. Over time, disappointment, disagreements, misunderstandings, busy schedules and lost opportunities can shatter our marital bliss. But it doesn't have to be that way. Relationships don't just fall apart one day. There are always signs – pretty common sense stuff that, when we neglect to consider in our relationships, invariably degenerates our bonds. But common sense is not always common, especially when emotions run high. *Lost Love* will help you identify and focus on the things (big and small) that can slowly tear your love apart – so that you know what warning signs to look for and to avoid. Plus, find out how to reignite your bruised relationship.

www.loveislost.com

Discriminate or Diversify: Those Who Can See
Through the Visible Can Achieve the Impossible!

Knowledge is power, and so is Diversity! Understanding and appreciating the unique differences that each race, sex, ethnicity, personality, age group, religion and other subcultures bring to the table will not only make you a more enlightened person and a more effective leader, but it can also boost your organization's bottom line (and *your* career) in a big way. In *Discriminate or Diversify*, Ruiz explores our history of discrimination, provides informed profiles on the many groups of people that make our world so interesting and exciting, and offers solutions for how to build a culture of Diversity and Inclusion in your organization. When you can see through the *visible*, you can achieve the impossible!

www.humandiversity.biz

www.ingramcontent.com/pod-product-compliance
Lightning Source LLC
Chambersburg PA
CBHW071053040426
42443CB00013B/3320